The Moon
And
The Nest

Published by
Apache Beach Publications
August, 2010

This novel is a work of fiction. Any references to historical events, to real people, living or dead, or to real locales are intended only to give the fiction a setting in historical reality. Other names, characters, places, and incidents, either are the product of the author's imagination or are used fictitiously, and their resemblance, if any, to real-life counterparts is entirely coincidental.

ISBN: 978-1-9302531-8-6

In Loving Memory of George Clark Chesbro

Chapter One

"So, what *are* you going to do for your next trick?" I could see George in my mind's eye waiting for a response; his patent steel blue eyes locking mine, a bit of a smirk on his face, and, as always, a vodka in hand. Still exceedingly angry with him, I didn't answer. "He that ain't busy being born is busy dying," he goaded me further. His persistence may have taken others by surprise but not me. Even dead he was a pit bull.

In all the years I'd watched him play out this little scenario with somebody *else* whose life had changed radically it was rare that he'd ever received an enthusiastic response; usually his question elicited a passionless shrug. As a result, and a sad commentary on both George's expectations and society's conforming demands, he'd lived close to twenty of his sixty-seven years as an unapologetic hermit, the author of twenty-five novels.

Now it was my turn to stand before George. He tried to reason with me constantly, for I was definitely 'busy dying.' Restless and rudderless, I could feel myself fading with each passing day. When one door closes another one opens? Maybe that's why I was wandering aimlessly from room to room, bouncing off the walls in the hope of finding that door - or at least the window. On and on came the barrage of boring little well-worn phrases people who loved me offered in consolation. They seeped into my head like so much sludge as I desperately searched for direction.

In the end it was the concept of freedom that reared its ugly head – obviously not the wonderful 'flag waving, glory days ahead' kind of freedom, but a rather unglamorous form that whispered insidiously in my ear. The stark reality of my life that freedom *was* just another word for nothing left to lose. When 49 years of loving George in one fashion or another was over, finished except for in my heart, it was this niggling little concept that motivated me to at least try to reverse the atrophy that was quickly becoming my life.

The only thought that bought me any peace was the idle musing of getting in my car and driving far, far away. Following the instinct to choose either fight or flight I wanted flight; for to continue living in the home we had created together, the home where George's presence was absent everywhere, seemed overwhelmingly depressing and unacceptable.

I permitted myself this harmless fantasy throughout the harsh New York winter months until I fell off the ladder stripping wallpaper in the bathroom and broke my left wrist, howling in pain more for the loss of George than the twisted misalignment I was holding in my right hand. My children, bless their loving souls, felt it was time for mamma to move close to them, and I knew damned well what this meant; the beginning of the end game of my life. Happy years in dotage watching grandchildren do handstands and maybe getting a part time job at a local bookstore.

My vision of driving far away intensified and a plan began to form like the tiny red embers of a new fire. I'd need a car bigger than my Accord so I could sleep in the back. 'Travel light travel far' was my motto, so there wouldn't have to be much storage space. Maybe one of those trucks with a cab would do; and since I was only going to travel in good weather areas why would I even need a heater? I continued to stoke the embers gently.

Our home in The Catskills sat triangulated in RV heaven. People came from all over the east coast to the area where we lived to buy motor homes. Surely I should check it out. Now a small fire had been started and I fed it constantly. In a guesstimate, the maximum length I would be able to comfortably handle was 25 feet - and I didn't want to pay much, either, so nothing new because I wasn't going to do this forever. Maybe two years. Maybe not two years. Maybe six months. But for now this was the only thing that made sense. As if anything made sense.

And then there was the practicality of driving something manageable. Handy was one thing, but it had to be middle-aged-woman user-friendly. Now *that's* a specification...

Sporting my game face I confidently took copious notes regarding the pros and cons of different models, sizes, price ranges, and various other sundry essentials for close to two months before, on what cringingly must be described as nothing short of a whim, I purchased a brand spanking new Class A Thor Hurricane. In my defense, it was an orphan from the previous year so I did get a great deal. All the other usual rationales of why this was the best choice for me followed suit, including an important safety feature - I could turn off the engine and go to bed without having to get outside of the cab. The fire was now raging inside me and it kept me warm.

Despite the motor home's masculine and

imposing name I had decided to call her The Nest. The Nest had two cream colored soft leather swivel chairs that when locked in a driving position perched on a ledge eight inches off the floor and faced the open road. Directly behind the chairs was a mushroom color carpeted area which could be greatly enlarged by electronically extending out both side walls when she was at rest. One nine foot extension had two benches that faced each other with a kitchen table between them that could be collapsed and made into a bed. Also part of that extension was a refrigerator, freezer and pantry. On the other side of the room was a couch which could be pulled out into a full bed. This area, about twelve feet in length extended to create a rather large living room with approximately seven feet between the seating. Behind this room was a kitchen, especially important because I liked my own cooking and, having rarely eaten out over the past eleven years, my digestive system became a bit finicky processing restaurant foods and downright rebellious regarding fast foods. The hall leading from the kitchen to the back area had a huge picture window on the right with nicely appointed day and night shades. There were two entrances to the bath. One from the hall on the left and the other from the back bedroom, accessed through a pocket door. The bedroom, itself, could be closed off via another pocket door that slid across at the end of the hall. Additionally, the bedroom was part of another, third, extension, very similar in size to the couch in the front.

The battery that started the engine also charged a second battery which provided inside energy for lighting. Additionally, there was a generator which ran from the seventy-five gallon gas tank that enabled me to use all of the electrical outlets, run the microwave, and provide alternate sources of energy for the refrigerator and hot water heater. The generator would automatically shut down if there was only a quarter tank of gas left, which would keep me from ever being stranded. These electrical options would be great in case I was situated where there was no electricity available; however, an electrical cord was kept in a back storage area under the body of the RV and, although thick and heavy, could provide me with 20, 30, or 50 amp service, depending upon what was available for me to plug into. A seventy-seven pound propane tank provided energy for heating the RV and the oven and stove, as well as an alternate source of energy for the refrigerator and hot water heater.

There was a connection for cable TV,

although the television and sound system were state of the art and an extendable antenna would certainly be enough for my needs.

A forty gallon fresh water tank, a forty gallon grey water tank (waste for shower and washing dishes), and a forty gallon dark water tank (toilet waste) further ensured that I could be without any dependency upon a campground for quite some time; going 'primitive' or 'boondoggling,' as it's called.

I was also happy to see an outside shower next to the water tanks.

She was not by any means perfect but I felt immediately maternal towards her; that is to say protective of, as well as protected in, my new home.

Aside from being 32 feet long, The Nest was twelve feet high and eleven feet wide. She was too big to tool around the cities or narrow streets so I purchased a Blue Ox tow so that my Accord, Maxine, could hum happily behind. The Blue Ox was a heavy accordion-like device that hooked to the back of the RV and onto a metal bar that had been placed inside Maxine and protruded out the front of her grill. Once connected, the accordion would expand and brace the two vehicles so that there wouldn't be any swerving. Just in case anything went wrong with the mechanism, I had two safety lines crisscrossed underneath the Blue Ox. Electrical wiring ran from under the hood of Maxine and was easily plugged into the back of The RV, ensuring my turn signals and stop lights worked on both the RV and Maxine.

With 185,000 miles under her belt, I wasn't worried about Maxine racking up additional miles but, after assurances that since she was a standard shift the mileage would be unaffected, it seemed that the plan was coming together nicely. So much for my motto 'travel light travel far'! Still, it felt right.

Now it was time for the precious cove on The Hudson River that had been our home, the land first hunted on by Mohican Indians, where later Dutch ship builders labored and then mushroom growers had lived to be gifted with love to its next inhabitants. A delightful young couple with three little boys bought the house, lock stock and barrel. Other than the clothes on my back and those few personal items I wished to take I didn't need to put furniture in storage or hold the mandatory garage sale - or estate sale, depending how fancy you are.

While the day of the house closing was an extraordinarily emotional day resplendent with torrential rains it was my intention to sit in calm; to be a part of everything that was happening and to let it happen without controlling, fear driven behaviors. All that could be done had been done. And, to that end, I must say it is amazing the amount of wonderful emotional gifts we receive when we let go. Pleased with the manner in which I occupied their children while they sifted through the volume of paperwork during the closing, the new owners had asked if I came with the house…

Later that same day The Nest officially became my new home and, determined to get paperwork and goodbyes in order as soon as I could possibly manage, I packed up my worldly goods and took two short dry runs with my dad. He was a wealth of helpful information which simply needed to be teased out of all of his unsolicited advice. Two weeks later I found myself driving, rather confidently, along The New York State Thruway through some of the most gorgeous countryside in the USA on my fifty-fifth birthday. Unplanned but perfect. It was as close to feeling satisfied, if not happy, as I had felt since before George left me. It made me chortle to think of how he would have hated going on such a journey. He abhorred taking any trip in a car that was over an hour long and, whining and whimpering he'd demand that I explain to his satisfaction what was so important about us leaving 'The Compound' in the first place.

When I had decided to go into Canada I cannot definitively say, but I remember thinking how wise it would be to explore more northern climes in the summertime and head south for the winter. I also liked the fact that it was a bit foreign to me. That is not to say I had never been there for a few weekends in Quebec or a short vacation once in Nova Scotia, but I had come to learn that if I had a strong thought then I should honor it as the right thing to do. Besides, there didn't seem to be any wrong thing to do.

I was proud to hand over my USA passport at the border kiosk to the handsome young man on duty. What is my business in Canada? Pleasure; I am eager to see your beautiful country! Do I have any weapons? Kitchen knives sprang to mind but I thought better of joking so shook my head seriously instead. I waited for him to instruct me to unlock the door and let him in. Perhaps he would admonish me for that open bottle of Chianti in the cupboard. But after looking at me with a trained eye he handed me back my passport, wished me a good trip and sent me on my way.

I've got that kind of trusting face. When I

meet someone for the first time one of two things happens. Either they think I look like their relative slash good friend slash high school buddy or they think I come from their country of origin. “Are you Irani?” “Are you French?” “You look just like my cousin, Ellen, who lives in Great Neck.” What I am is a product of the USA melting pot. I tend to be a natural pacer, too, picking up dialect and idiomatic expressions, as they feel happy on my tongue. I’m glad I appeared non-threatening to the customs border officer, but hoped I could appear very threatening to an emotionally unhealthy person who might be looking to disturb my peace.

Chapter Two

It felt comforting to have seen the nice big fat question mark on a welcoming sign as I entered The Province of Ontario. Despite how organized I'd tried to be the last eight months, I was still barely putting one foot in front of the other - spending just enough time to make sure that the foot I was setting down was landing on a stable step. Other than seeing the name "Hamilton" written next to a dot on Lake Ontario on my USA map, I wasn't sure where to go or what the procedures were for provincial parks. Hamilton spoke to me only because I hoped to lie quietly on a natural body of water for a bit and, based on the map's key, it appeared to be about a 45 minute drive over the border. Close enough to feel I'd arrived. Or left.

The Information Center in Ontario was a busy, friendly place and two lovely women vied for my attention, bubbling with enthusiasm and pride about their grand Province. They gave me a map and happily they concurred that I would love The Hamilton Beach Wildlife Conservancy.

Within the hour I exited The Queen's

Expressway and quickly came upon the wooded area clearly marked, which, as advertised, abutted the sandy shores of Lake Ontario. Relieved and almost giddy with anticipation, I slid open the driver's side window and sang out to the cherub face with freckles that had popped her head out of the official welcoming kiosk, "I'm so happy to be here!"

"We're so happy to have you here!" She chirped back. Reservation book in hand she asked, "What is your name?"

"Oh, I don't have a reservation." My voice trailed but I then added hopefully, "The women at the Information Center recommended this campground to me just an hour ago."

"Sure," she laughed a little disdainfully, looking at my New York State license plate. "I'll bet they didn't tell you this weekend is The Civic Holiday, either."

'Either' obviously meaning she didn't have a site for me. I will warrant you that I barely keep up with my own holidays but I'd never even *heard* of The Civic Holiday. Here I was only six hours from where I used to call home and I was beginning to realize that, other than language, I had entered an unknown culture. What lousy timing! The cherub must have seen my face drop and, as a cherub must, she took pity on my

predicament.
"Park over there," she spoke commandingly and pointed to the right side of the entrance. "Come inside and I'll see what I can do."
Already shaking, but trying to keep a stiff upper lip I parked where she had indicated and made my way into the small brown office.
By the time I'd stepped up to the counter she had already reconnoitered her charges. "I have a spot that won't open until five o'clock tonight and you can stay there, but just for this one night."
I could have kissed her. After thanking her profusely she questioned me in more detail. "How long are you going to be in Ontario?"
"I don't know, but I'm hoping to travel across Canada over the next few months."
"Splendid," she effused, "but first you've got to find a spot for this weekend. The Civic Holiday is similar to your Labor Day weekend. It will be very difficult to find any place to stay. I suggest you go as far north and away from Toronto as you can. Try Sturgeon Bay. It's small and a lot of people don't know about it." She wrote the number down on a piece of scrap paper.
Grateful for the information and determined to handle one problem at a time, I paid my $30.00 fee through teary eyes and headed back to The Nest to make that call for a

reservation further up the pike, happy I had changed my phone service to an international status.

There was a cocoon-like feeling to The Nest when all the curtains were pulled. It afforded me privacy while, still parked on the entrance, I was able to change into a bathing suit before heading out to the beach. Toronto, directly to the north across The Great Lake could be seen at night I'd been told, but on this hot hazy day puffy pink pillows of clouds hung lazily in a powder blue sky that blended into Ontario's horizon. Shades of soft ceruleans confused my ability to see where sky ended and waters began. As I walked through the pebbly beach into the water I was struck by the silence. There was even a 'no cell-phone' sign. Closing my eyes and feeling full in the moment that I was part of I had to smile. It wasn't silent at all! Ducks were chattering away madly, almost drowning out the sound of soughing waves. A distant train said 'hello' and, although the beach was empty, people were joyous in their celebration not very far away. Amazing what we *don't* hear going on around us! I took two quick dunks to fulfill the requirement for having been in Lake Ontario and, not that I wouldn't have loved a big swim, but I became oddly concerned about my body's ability to fight foreign

bacteria.
As I began walking back to The Nest I saw a man sitting on a bench that had been strategically positioned for a panoramic view of The Great Lake. Slightly balding on top, his shoulder length wheat gray hair softly responded to the gentle breezes. With his arm slung over the back of the bench I had a clear view of his side profile. Perhaps it was his dreamy expression or easy posture, one leg crossed over the other, but he looked exactly like George on one of his last book jacket covers. I put his age at about 45 and so began the backward count. Now, let's see, when George was 45 how old was I? I played this little game in my head all the time. Well, I was 31. My daughter, Rachael, was six. In four more years we would visit George so that she could write her fourth grade report about a local author. How gracious and humble he had been. How lucky we were to have such a fine friend of the family! It was always so exciting to be in his presence. Ever since I was a little girl he appeared to me to be such a shining star…
The walk back to The Nest seemed much longer, and much hotter than the walk to the beach had been. I could feel the pebbles on the gravelly road through the soles of my cheap, thin flip flops. What I needed was a

thorough, soapy shower and a nap.

As the sun softened the late day I too began to release tension and decided that, as long as I returned from dinner while it was still daylight, it would be fun to eat at the marina restaurant I'd passed on my way to the beach. A lot had happened today. It was easy to forget that it was my birthday. After my nap I popped on a long cotton shift before putting on a little makeup and, as always, my wedding ring before heading out to the marina.

Sailboats and power boats alike bobbed happily alongside the maze of docks. Unsure of how to get from point A to point B, I flagged down a man and woman walking on the shoreline.

"Excuse me. Sorry to bother you, but could you tell me how to get to the restaurant?"

"Sure," responded the heavily accented man. He was eager to be of assistance and, tossing a thumb in the woman's direction added, "Jill, here's headed over there for a drink. I have to ready the boat. We're headed ouuuut to Toronto Island tonight to celebrate The Holiday."

Ah, The Holiday!

After official introductions Bob, Jill and I walked, or rather bounced, along the floating docks like old salts until we reached The Marina Restaurant at which point I felt comfortable to ask Jill, a very pleasant, handsome blond woman, if I might join her in that drink. Agreeable, we parted company from Bob and took a small table on the veranda. We both ordered Absolute - straight up with olives.

I had already learned on our walk to the restaurant that Jill was visiting from Calgary. She and her sister, Bob's wife, were meeting a third sister for the weekend. She had already learned that I recently lost my husband.

"What do you do in Calgary?"

"Well…" She seemed hesitant.

I sat quietly and she started again.

"I'm recently divorced. Eighteen months." She stabbed at the olives in her drink ruefully. "What else… I've got a part time job but it's not much."

"Boy, I remember when I got divorced. Married almost twenty years."

"Me, too….twenty-two years."

We divorcees carry the number like some kind of third place plastic trophy in bowling. Her eyes met mine and I recognized the sorrow.

"I never thought I would be happy again, Jill," I shared with her. "I thought at *most* I would be content, and that would have to be enough. But then came George." I smiled brightly. "He was a gift I could not deny myself."

"So there's hope... for love..." Jill said it haltingly, as if she didn't want to jinx it, as if saying it out loud would or would not make it so.

That was as far as our little burgeoning conversation got, for Bob came upon us as quick as the dark clouds overhead.

"We've got to get going, *now*." The urgency in his voice was unmistakable.

We said our hurried goodbyes and hugged, wishing each other well. It was as if the winds themselves were ripping us apart as she and Bob flew off to the boat, hoping to beat out the impending storm.

I decided against dinner and finished Jill's drink after my own before scurrying back to The Nest.

That night as the rains beat on the roof of my home I laid in bed musing over my very first day and my conversation with Jill.

*

"I'd like to hold you. Would you like to be held?" He had asked me that crisp autumn Sunday afternoon. Now, I'd known George through two wives and more women than I had fingers and toes to count with, but no alarm bells went off in my head to warn me. Not a one, for I could see he had changed. As a result of his philandering and a rather queer brain he'd been living as a hermit on

The Hudson River in Nyack, New York without even owning a car and had written a total of 20 novels in as many years. In this self-imposed exile George had learned to heal himself.

Having said that, I'd felt so shy to 'it all." I was a free agent, I'd told myself. I wanted to be with him, but I had been with only one man for the past twenty-some years. Also, I'm a bonder. No getting around it, if I went to bed with this man it would be serious for me. Already thin and fragile after the divorce, I could very easily have my heart broken…

Sometime later that first night I felt George pull away from me and get out of the tiny single bed. He padded into the kitchen directly across from the little room and opened up the French doors that led to a small, rickety deck. He poured himself a glass of vodka and had a cigarette, listening to the waves of The Hudson River crash on the rocks below us. I knew he was sorry that we had gone to bed together. It was a mistake for a man who lived alone, deliberately shunning human connections, to bed a friend who did not understand his reclusive and quirky, compulsive ways. I cowered against the wall, glad the broken bed slanted in that direction and sadly waited while he figured out how to carefully word the verdict. When he crawled back into the bed, frozen to the bone, he held me like a bear holds its cub, stroking my hair as he spoke. "For so many, many years I have been content living alone, feeling that love had been burnt out of me - and been glad for it. Feeling that my life was close to being over and that it was alright. But some mornings I'd wake up from a deep night's sleep and *know* I felt love, if only in my dreams. I just could never see who it was. It was you, Robin. I have loved you in my dreams and I will not let my fears ruin this chance for happiness. If we can both trust what we are feeling now I know that I'll be entering the most joyous period of my life." Residual light from a street lamp softly lit our faces through the filthy window of the miserable hovel he'd called 'home'. I could tell from his reaction that he saw the adoration in my eyes.

*

The next morning I woke to sunshine and comfortably unhooked my 20 amp electric and the water hose. Less confidently, I put on my gloves and carefully disassembled the sewer hose. After reviewing my fifteen point check list I started up The Nest and carefully pulled out of my site, stopping at the office to drop off a bottle of wine with

The Cherub of Check In before winding my way back to The Queens Expressway. An hour later I was sitting in bumper to bumper traffic reminiscent of The Garden State Parkway in New Jersey on a Friday night before The Fourth of July weekend. I stayed in one lane and paid close attention for the next four miserable, hot hours. By about one p.m., I realized I didn't know how far north it would be this tied up and that my reservation might not be saved. I hit 'redial' and on the third ring heard a most pleasant voice.

"Sturgeon Bay Provincial Park, Ranger Richard speaking."

"Well, good afternoon, Ranger Richard. This is Robin Chesbro calling. I didn't know how long you held reservations for, but I am stuck on the QEW and am not sure *when* I will arrive."

"Miss Chesbro, we don't take reservations."

I'm lucky I didn't hit the car in front of me.

"No. No, I spoke with Jason yesterday afternoon and he told me he had two 'pull-throughs' left. I gave him my name and I *thought* I even gave him my phone number."

There was silence.

Then there was begging. "Ranger Richard, I am so sorry to cause a problem, but I just came into Canada yesterday, completely unaware of the holiday. Is there

anything…"
"No, I'm sorry. We have nothing available."
I waited one more small hopeful moment. Then it came.
"I will find a spot for you. You won't have any hook up, but…"
"Oh, that's alright! Just a place to park the RV and sleep is all I need!" I promised. "Thank you, thank you, sir. And I'm sorry for the miscommunication. I thought for sure the young man was writing down my information…."
Ranger Richard obviously knew the young teenager who had been manning the phones yesterday for he had an unmistakable apologetic tone when he replied, "I'm sorry for the miscommunication, too. Where are you now?"
I gave him the name of the last sign I'd seen, "Painswick."
"It will open up by Barrie," he assured me. We'll see you about four.
"Thank you, Ranger Richard. Thank you so much. I will see you then."
The man was a god to me at that moment. The fact that I had another three hours of driving was dwarfed by the fact that I would be alright. One day at a time. One foot in front of the other. I vowed that this would be the last time I'd experience my trip in

such a slipshod manner and determined to be better prepared going forward.

At ten to four I stepped out of The Nest and into the sunlight at Sturgeon Bay. Now personally, I hate sturgeons. They are warty bottom feeders and many a stream along the hi-ways and bi-ways of the Hudson River proudly featured a sign with a picture of the grossly malformed mascot beneath; *Kill - Sturgeons* it would read. "Good!" I would exclaim, jokingly, reading the Dutch word for stream, kill, as a call to arms instead. Well, from this day forward the sturgeon would be forever known to me as much beloved.

Despite the dozen or so people waiting to be assigned their spots, Ranger Richard identified me immediately. I imagine he's quite used to that 'deer in the headlights' look, but I was touched that a man, so obviously busy on The Great Civic Holiday (although it was called The Civic Holiday, I had taken to increasing its status) would take the time for such individual kindness. For my part, Ranger Richard was a made for movie icon. A kind of a Tom Selleck ruggedness with softer features. He looked at me for recognition and I broke into a wide smile. "Ranger Richard?"

"Ms. Chesbro?"

I nodded, too grateful or exhausted to speak.

I wasn't sure which.
"Let me show you where I can put you up for the night. You might not want it." He said, shaking my outstretched hand.
I choked back the mad laughter. "I'm very grateful, wherever it is."
Ranger Richard drove his shiny white pickup truck for me to follow, leading me around the inner loop of the campground so that I could head The Nest and Maxine in the right direction. The grounds were packed and there was not a square inch that wasn't occupied. Hoards of day campers lounged lazily on the beach.
Across the street from the campground was an RV storage area behind a small store where many motor homes were kept, some wrapped in blue polymer prophylactics. Under the trees to the right of the two acre lot was a flat stretch of grass next to swamp-like thrushes. Approximately 150 yards away were three little rental cabins with the day's sandy towels and bathing suits slung over the railings. I wouldn't be completely alone.
"What do you think?" He asked.
"Perfect, Ranger Richard." I had begun to say his name with an affectionate lilt.
"Well, then, after you've set yourself up come back to the office and we'll register you."

All this and I would be an official guest, too! After disconnecting Maxine and backing into the spot, I quickly threw on a bathing suit and a cover-up before pulling a bottle of Valpolicello out of the cabinet. Thanking with wine was becoming a habit.

By five thirty I had registered and was laying on the beach thinking, once again, that in life it was better to be lucky than good. The solitude in the storage area suited me and, perhaps foolishly, I did not feel afraid. After all, Ranger Richard was watching out for me!

The feeling of euphoria did not last through the night. It must have been something I ate. Or perhaps the water. I would have left in the morning and driven further north, but Ranger Richard had seemed pleased that I was pleased and so the next morning I weakly dragged myself over to the office and asked, humbly, if I could spend another night in 'The Annex'. Partly amused by my affections for the seedy grounds I'm sure, Ranger Richard acquiesced.

"I saw you driving around at 8 p.m. last night and again at 7 a.m. this morning," his shiny white pickup truck impossible to miss. "Do you live here in season?"

"Oh, no," he said with a broad smile. "I drive about a half hour north and then take a

boat out to my island every night. I have a cottage there."
"Really!" That sounded fabulous. "Are you here all winter?"
"No, I have a daughter in Verne and I visit with her when I shut down the cottage before the bay freezes."
I noticed he wasn't wearing a wedding ring.
"My husband and I lived on The Hudson River for many years. He was a writer and I paint." I offered, then added lightly, "I'm a water rat, too!"
He laughed at the visualization.
On impulse I grabbed some literature off the walls and set out, hoping a little walk would help right my digestive system. A lovely retired couple let me join them in their morning constitution. They were knowledgeable about the area and proud to share. It seems I had stumbled onto a Biosphere Reserve. The eastern coast of Georgian Bay on Lake Huron had been designated by UNESCO as the world's largest fresh water archipelago, consisting of thirty thousand islands. Sharon and Blair had been coming to Sturgeon Bay every year for the past twenty-five years, reserving their site on-line the very first hour that the Ontario Provincial Park permitted, seven months before each camping season started. When their children grew up, got married,

and had children of their own, the number of sites they reserved increased. They waved to sons, daughter-in-laws, grandchildren and friends they'd made during their annual pilgrimage as we walked throughout the park. Having invested in a small boat years before, they fished and poked around the islands during the day. Their nights were spent with family around the campfire, cooking the fruits of their labors and singing. They very generously made me feel at home in their world, sharing much about themselves and showing concern for my well being.
I have always enjoyed being alone and, while I missed my mate, I had never felt lonely. This encounter, however, was the first of many during which I realized how much I appreciated kindnesses of others and my own desire to fight against alienation. Sharon and Blair spent their winters in Texas, graciously giving me contact information so that I might visit them there during my southern travels. I actually thought I might.

Feeling less intestinally challenged but still wary, I had taken to boiling water. Despite protestations by anyone to the contrary I felt I just couldn't take the chance. As I sat at my kitchen table while the day turned to diurnal I saw movement out of the corner of my eye. Moving slowly so as not to scare the two creatures, I watched intently. Deeper into the thrushes they moved, murmuring softly to each other. After observing the sweet scene for a few moments longer my curiosity got the better of me.

"What are you boys hunting for?" My voice was soft so as not to disturb them. Both were hooded and, moving stealthily themselves, carried their nets in readiness to pounce upon their prey. The tiny faces twisted quickly to me, shock and a little fear in their eyes. They were about ten and I'd scared them. I was immediately sorry.

The taller boy got his voice first. "Tree frogs. There's loads of them in here."

"Really?" I asked, impressed to be included… as far as it went.

"Yeah," the shorter boy added, "We caught like, maybe ten last year."

"Wow, that's great," I continued in a whisper. "Well, good luck, fellas." I said and slid my kitchen window back shut.

A moment later the boys left the thrushes to head off to pastures less inhabited. How wondrous to be young and on an adventure!

That night I toyed with the possibility of staying another night, as Monday was the official holiday and the roads would be, again, packed, although probably not northbound. I had a few glasses of wine and listened to some fine music. I thought about Ranger Richard. I drank some more wine. I wondered if Ranger Richard might come over to 'check on me.' I climbed into bed and started sketching some of the sights I had seen from the bay, imagining that the campground must seem like a poor sister to him, compared with his haven. I'm sure he couldn't wait to sit on his porch each night and watch the setting sun, a glass of Valpolicello in hand. The attraction I was feeling toward him was strong, but I'm not a fool. I understood full well it was The Canadian Mounties Syndrome; Dudley Dooright to the rescue on his white Ford, saving the distressed maiden and all. Yet even deliberately demystifying the feeling, I still couldn't deny that it was happening. I imagined living on that little island, wind blowing through my hair, and of course, while I was imagining, Ranger Richard was a phenomenal lover.

My reverie was broken when I turned and faced a picture of George and me on the end table. We were on The Angel Trail at The Grand Canyon some ten years earlier. He was sitting comfortably on a flat, broad rock wearing one of his Marlboro baseball caps and smiling broadly. I was squatting beside

him, with matching cap and smile.
Despite his easy demeanor in the picture, George was brusque and dismissive to me. “I’m dead,” he said, “Move on.”
I was horrified. “Fuck You, George!” I yelled back. “Fuck you and don’t you *dare* say that again.” Hot, angry tears were streaming fast, dropping like hail on my sketch pad. “You have no fortitude. That’s your problem. You gave up too easy. You don’t have my determination. You are *weak* and I hate you!”
As furious as I was with him, I couldn’t help but notice how soft the skin on his neck was and how magnificently carved his hands were. Eventually the tears slowed down.
“Don’t say that, again.” I begged him lovingly and ending all further conversation on the matter.

The next morning tons of campers were buzzing around the office as if samples of honey were being given out.
“What’s going on?” I asked a teenage girl.
“My grandpa caught a rattle snake and the Ranger’s gone to get it.”
A moment later Ranger Richard flanked by two of his teenage interns came walking up the path with a thirty gallon plastic garbage can in one hand and a long rod-type thing in his other. We all gathered around to receive

the eco-lesson. Everyone stood quietly, peeking over the rim as close as we dared and listening to the soft purring sound the three foot long rattlesnake was making.

"This is a Massauga rattle snake." He informed the small, rapt crowd.

I filed away the rattle snake's genus under 'Shock and Awe.'

"Only two people have died in the last sixty years from this type of snake bite," he taught us. "And that's because they didn't go to the hospital for treatment."

We all nodded. Two was a reasonable rate.

The rattlesnake purred insistently, "Don't believe him!" He seemed to be saying, "I'm deadly poison!!"

We backed away from the rim, unsure who to trust.

"This little guy is pretty large, for a Massauga, but you really don't have to worry if you come across them I the wild. They are more afraid of us than we are of them."

Eyes narrowed further.

He didn't seem to have much else to tell us, so Ranger Richard stood by quietly and let us all have a good gander until eventually interest in the 'little guy' waned and the crowd began to dissipate.

Still uncertain whether I should stay another day or leave, I hung around hoping for

inspiration.
I went back over to the snake, but it had no further revelations.
"What will you do with him?" I asked Ranger Richard.
"Oh, I'm going to wait about an hour and then set him lose behind the office," he told me with a wry smile.
I had to laugh.
"We *all* live here, you know."
Of course he was right.
"Are you staying another day?" He asked with no particular inflection that I could ascertain.
"No." I answered softly, not taking my eyes off the striations on the snake. "I think I'll head up toward Chute."
"Killarney is also very beautiful, especially if you paint." He said helpfully.

Chapter Three

The drive north was gray and sad. I made two terrible miscalculations while driving. Once I pulled into traffic and did not put the 'pedal to the metal' as hard and as fast as I should have. Cars behind me needed to break. I could see from my rear view camera that nobody had swerved, but we all got real close. I could live with that and I'm sure it has long since been forgotten by the victims of my stupidity. Hell, I've rolled my eyes at plenty of assholes on the road and, honestly, navigating something the length and heft of The Nest and Maxine combined was turning me into a more compassionate driver.

The second transgression was more serious. In an attempt to cheer myself up, I had plugged the tiny ipod into the auxiliary outlet of my radio so that I didn't have to put on the ear plugs and was listening to my favorite 'hot stuff' come over the great sound system. While I love all kinds of music, the last several months I'd been in a real jag of hip hop and rap. I had decided that it was the great Eros life drive that drew me to the primal, simple beats and singing at the top of my lungs I crooned, "You spin me right round baby, right round, like a record baby right round, round, round, round!" It definitely activated my pheromones. The fact that that particular song was a twenty year old remake had been completely lost on my daughters' friends, who held the music as their own and to whom I looked like a cool middle aged chick to even know of its existence. I'd seen some of the videos and I found them to be very evocative, as well. Not just sexually provocative, which they were, but viscerally stirring and they made me happy. In the way that operas and symphonies brought me to the depths of my emotions and the harsh reality of my loss, rap and hip hop was having the exact opposite effect.

While driving The Nest I had gotten into a habit of putting my left foot on the dashboard. It relieved pressure off my back and just felt good. What I had forgotten was that the right and left side view mirrors were adjusted electronically from that spot and I had not locked the small lever into a 'hold' position. My foot had slid over and activated the control for the right view mirror, angling it out to an area further to my right. And, distracted by the music, I hadn't even heard it happen. About ten minutes later I put on my right blinker to give plenty of notice to the general vicinity of drivers that I was going to get off the next exit. The car in the right hand lane was too far back to be seen through the shadeless window over my right shoulder, the bottom curved side view mirror placed it *very* far behind me, and the top right side view mirror was, well, giving me a clear picture of The QEW's shoulder, not the right hand lane I was moving into. I am so grateful that I didn't hit the car I had cut off and that the other driver had the wherewithal to be as defensive as we all know we should be. It wasn't even that I was in a rush to get off the exit or had miscalculated the time it would take me to get there. It was a mistake I would never make again and it drove home, once again, the precariousness and fragility of life; that everything could be over in a second. I was responsible for a huge piece of equipment on the roads and, after everything I had prided myself in learning about her, if I wasn't uber-cautious The Nest could be an instrument of disaster due to overconfidence.

I got off the exit at Killarney and saw from the sign that it was approximately forty miles south. My nerves had been so jostled due to my incompetence that I lost heart to venture off the main drag. I gassed up at $4.40 a gallon, took a pee and got back on The QEW. Even the shocked and admiring

looks I'd gotten from people at the gas station who realized I was soloing my journey did not perk up my spirits.
When I arrived at Chute I was dog tired. Low and slightly disoriented I pulled in, plugged in, and climbed in to bed.

*

George believed he was the product of clanky genes, considering his childhood a 'grey' period. Gauging from the school notes his mother had kept from his teachers, he was a very difficult child as well. To quote one, "George is going to hell in a hand basket and taking half the class with him." Probably testosterone helped because by the time he hit high school he'd become Captain of the Swim Team and been elected Class President. George felt, perhaps apocryphally, that his parents had rooted for his opponent. By the time he was in college, however, his outward confidence broke. He'd suffered what we would probably now consider a nervous breakdown. Always a mediocre student, he'd had very low self esteem and felt much of his life was beyond his control. The little worlds he created when he wrote, however, he could control. Additionally, by calling himself a writer he was a 'somebody'. Ten years later when he published his first poem for a buck he began to tout his greatest strength as being perverse perseverance. This trait eluded him when it came to women.

I, on the other hand, was a 'perfect' child…the oldest of eight. My mother suffered from severe depression and childhood abuse and my father suffered from a Messianic complex, setting out to create his version of The Kennedys. I was a competent caretaker but determined early on that Roman Catholicism and mental distress were a combustible combination that I could not be part of and opted, by the time I was twenty, for Conservadox Judaism. I thrived in the social connectedness, becoming President of The Sisterhood of Monsey Jewish Center, a six hundred family shul - and yes, it is true what they say that if you have ten Jews you've got twelve opinions - I loved it! I became the director for a national health care company and other assorted 'power mamma' positions, living a productive, materialistic, judgmental life. Outwardly loving and compassionate, inwardly repressed and restless. Then the bottom dropped out. My mother's eight year affair with, and subsequent law suit against, the parish priest made front page news for eight days. My father's exposure of my mother's depression- induced behaviors was a secret I was not prepared to relinquish. Within a week I was in much needed therapy and subsequently developed a vocabulary to explain what happened and, more importantly for the first time, how I felt about it. I don't know how else to explain it other than to say that my brain rewired. This destabilized an otherwise perfectly amenable marriage and within three years I, too, was divorced.

There were three common denominators that drew George and I to each other. First, we both considered ourselves spiritual warriors and believed that all religions were, while probably genetically wired, limiting the advancement of the species. You don't make many friends with this ideology and we were, generally speaking, careful not to share our views, for believers in deities find this concept frightening and threatening. Creating and recreating ourselves daily, we tried to live in appreciation for the mysteries of the universe without feeling the need to have all the answers. Secondly, we needed very little. Materialistically as well as from others. I was now free to love my family and friends without needing them to behave in a certain way for me to be alright. George loved, but was emotionally disconnected from, his family. We both believed that understanding and having compassion for our emotions as well as healing life's humiliations and hurts were the key to individual and then in turn collective growth. Thirdly, we both loved sex. I'll say no more.

*

I woke to another gray morning. Poor Ontario was having probably the worst summer on record between the rain and cold weather. I'd understood it was because The North Atlantic Oscillation created an abnormal high pressure area which was keeping the jet stream of warm, southern Pacific winds from coming into the Provinces. I still hadn't put on a pair of shorts. The next few days of driving were grueling and I felt as if I were slogging through a mental fog as well as a topographical one. Each morning I woke to one recurring theme. The one thing I could be sure of was that this day would be completely different from yesterday. Not knowing what to expect could be exciting but it could also be unnerving. Upon waking I would do my best to center myself spiritually and resolve to move forward with a 'good attitude'.

Lake Superior was as dark and active as a sea. Its bluish grey-green crashing waves were so unique that The Lake cannot be mistaken for any other of The Great Lakes. It presented itself to me, hitting the horizon on one of my darkest days. Clouds seemed bottomless as they rushed by on their way to deposit even more rain to the east. Up and down I drove, Superior to my left, escarpments to my right. The tachometer read five thousand as the engine raced madly to keep up with the demand. We climbed higher and higher only to be breaking frantically down the steep declines. The next dot on the map this morning was WaWa. Billboards advertised the treasures we would be rewarded with if we kept at it. It would take two and a half hours into my four hour travel for the day, so WaWa seemed to be the perfect stop for a break in driving, but when I got there I was in shock at the site. Clearly the signs had outlived the town, as motel after gas station after restaurant was boarded up and desolate. I kept moving.

I'd left Saulte Sainte Marie at 8:30 a.m. and Greta Garmin's estimated time of arrival at The White Lake Provincial Campground was noon. Although my upper back was getting stiffer as the days passed and it was becoming increasingly important for me to stretch out, arriving at my destination at a decent hour would give me a full afternoon to take a good long walk. Additionally, my stomach had been acting up again despite boiling water I knew I was going to have to start buying bottled water. There was a nauseating taste of metal in my mouth and I had been thinking the worst. I passed up an opportunity to gas up in an area because it was packed with buses, RVs, trucks and car caravans, hoping there would be another less crowded station up ahead. I pressed on, unrewarded, and reached The White Lake Provincial Campgrounds with a quarter of a tank of gas. Now, a generous guesstimate of a quarter tank is twenty gallons which would offer any car driver comfort, but at seven miles to the gallon, that would be cutting it close driving through such undeveloped areas. Too close for me to relax about it. I paid the pretty teenage girl with pink skunk-striped hair and short chipped yellow nails with blue tips the standard $32.50.

"No cell service," she happily reported.

Depending upon my phone in case of a real emergency had always offered me tremendous comfort in traveling alone. I asked, "But what if something serious happens. 911 works, right?"

"Nope. You'll have to come down here to make the call."

The idiocy of such a statement eluded her. I didn't respond.

The roads were very narrow and the trees overgrown, scrapping across my bow. At one point I thought I would have to

disconnect Maxine as it looked to be a dead end up ahead. Thank goodness for the kind and knowledgeable encouragement from fellow campers who were shocked to see I had been sent back there. It took me a solid twenty minutes to wind my way back to the campground office where, with as steady a voice as I could muster, I asked for a refund. "Yeah," she said with a conspiratorial nod of the head, "I think it's a little narrow down there for something your size." She then added in afterthought, "I think I should go down there and see how it's laid out."
A case of bad nerves coming to the fore, I began to throw my fears out about the possibility of a gas station up ahead into the mix of conversation. She *absolutely* assured me that there *probably* was something further west within the hour. I'm sure she said more but I was gone. Now, having no idea where I would stay for the night and feeling that I could last another hour driving, tops, I climbed back on the roost and fought back the tears. "Don't you dare cry," I chastised myself. "This is NOT a problem! You are letting your fears get the best of you. Breath and calm down." It wasn't easy.

Thirty minutes later I was fully gassed up. Nothing inspires confidence like a full tank.

I was determined to remember this feeling and first, not let the tank get much below half for my own sanity and second, not be so frightened about what was up ahead, or not up ahead, the next time I needed to make a change in plans. We'll see how that works out...

A quick glance at the Ontario Parks map put Neys about twenty-five minutes more west. If it was like White Lake I couldn't stay but; there I was worrying again.

I almost cried with relief to see a knowledgeable staff and beautiful grounds - wide and welcoming. I followed the easy directions to a pull-through, gratefully taking the 15 volt electric offered. Did I hear soughing of waves through the copse of fir directly ahead? Despite my exhaustion I ran to see. Indeed! Brilliant beaches littered with white washed logs and other assorted flotsam - a naturist's dream!

Like I said earlier, a lousy beginning can end up great. You just never know what the day will bring.

*

I thought that George was going to kill me. Literally.

Despite the fact he had insisted I bought him at a yellow toe tag sale from the dusty fields behind the Sex Slave Academy. He'd said

I'd turned up my nose at all of the young, tanned and well oiled sex slaves rotating on the glittering silver pedestals during the Annual Academy Presentation. Imagining my attendance at the extravaganza like that of Cleopatra, including being carried by slaves on my barge, I was bored with the participants, he'd said. Then, just as I was about to leave I had caught George out of the corner of my eye.

"I'll take HIM!" I'd exclaimed to the handlers. I took him home and had him scrubbed up and that is the story of how George became my sex slave.

I called him my luscious and lascivious lamb legs.

He said I would always be the spring chicken.

I promised to keep him young forever.

He said I was his sex sorceress.

He told my daughters that they should forget all notions of finding a man to marry and that what they really needed was good, reliable sex slave in order to live a happy life.

The man took his responsibilities seriously and did not want to be put back into the dusty fields ever again and I thought that he was going to give me a heart attack proving himself worthy.

*

I decided to stay in Neys for two days during which time my nausea subsided and I received a wonderful history lesson. Neys, in Ashburton, was the site where high ranking German officers were kept prisoners of war during World War II. The reclusiveness of the choice aside, as I stood on the beach I couldn't help but reflect on their reality. No matter how magnificent and bucolic the setting it was a prison to these men. There was a little museum dedicated to their 'stay', which I strolled through leisurely. Many enlarged black and white photos of smiling men standing together, boxing tournaments, pictures of a man beside his art work, probably taken for propaganda purposes, seemed to imply they were comrades enjoying good times together. I couldn't help but be disgusted recalling how horrifically their compatriots had been treating our 'side'. And, to that end, I was not shocked to learn that after being sent back to Germany to be with their families many of the men had returned to either visit or live here in Ashburton when the war was over.

The three hour drive from Neys to Thunder Bay was spectacular. Having left the campground at 7:00 a.m., I was witness to an impressive morning show. Thousands of yards of gauzy scrim fog lay thickly on all of the many lakes. With more lakes than words to name them, by the time I came to Lake Mom I was smiling. When I saw Lake Baby I grinned. By the time I crossed over Lake Dad I had to laugh out loud. The maze of rivers and streams connected with a logic known only to themselves. I had determined to take life easy today, despite the fact that I was unsure what to expect after a scheduled stop in Thunder Bay. It was time for The Nest's mandatory check up and arrangements had been made to change the oil and filter at a dealership in Thunder Bay. How long would it take? Would I have energy to travel further or be emotionally exhausted from whatever else the mechanics might 'find' wrong? My concerns were ill founded and I was back on the road headed towards Kakabeka Falls by 11:30.

Just six inches! Six lousy inches and my 30 amp cable would have reached the campground outlet. Sure, I tried wiggling the RV with the car still attached, but I just couldn't get close enough. And sure, I could have lived with 15 amps, but finally the cold spell had broken and I was positioned for a day in the hot sun. I wanted to use my air conditioner and for that I would need the 30 amp. Well, the girls who registered me at the front gate assured me that, while the spot was tight, if I had difficulty approaching from the left I was free to circle around on the one way street and approach the site from the opposite direction. After hemming and hawing for about an hour I realized there would be no peace until I shut myself up, so I started the RV and with Maxine in tow, began the circle to reconnoiter. Heading down the narrow way I heard the unmistakable sound of metal on bark. In my attempt to 'circle wide' - the mantra of us right turning RVers, I neglected to notice a birch tree on the road's edge of the driver's side. Arrrrgghhh! My awning! Immediately I assured myself that I'd always hated the thing anyway. It had obviously made to be 'comfortably maneuvered' by two people, both of whom would have to be over six foot tall. I had never put it up. Arduously and extremely careful (now) I began to back up, watching with baited breath as the tires on Maxine begin to twist malevolently, for angled too strongly they will just skid sideways. It became crystal clear to me that the turn I was hoping to take would be impossible. I made a left, instead, and despite the fact that I could hear a bottle rolling around the kitchen floor I pressed on. Who cared what the hell that was; I had bigger fish to fry! I drove approximately a quarter of a mile down the wrong way of a one lane path hoping no one would come in from the other direction at this particular time and raising my hand in mea culpa for all other campers to see. I know! I know! Twenty lashes with a wet noodle! As the circumstances began to lighten it occurred to me that it was not my awning, but the protective water-wicking roll-up over my largest extension that had gotten into consternation with the birch! What if it was broken permanently? Well, nothing to do at this moment but get to safety. After pulling back into my site and shutting the engine I turned around to see exactly what had been rolling around the kitchen floor. A previously corked two liter bottle of Shiraz, the colorful kangaroo on the label now sitting in a puddle of purple, had splattered on the carpet, the couch, and all over the kitchen floor. Triage! I grabbed for paper towels and Spot Shot.

"What a misery! You need eyes in the back of your head, which is why people don't do this alone!!" I scrubbed and sprayed and cursed. My head felt like it would burst. My back stiffened up again, but, the inside mess now cleaned up, I had to see what damage had been done to the extension. Ladder and broom in hand I proceeded to the scene of the crime for an inspection. Gingerly I brushed away pieces of bark and leaves. There was a small marking where the protective cover had been slightly hole-pocked but it had not ripped. It seemed as though one of the holding rods had been pushed further out of its socket than the other side of the cover. I ran to the other front extension to compare the two arms and saw that they were lined up exactly the same. Thank goodness! Back inside, I opened a side window so that I could monitor the situation while very slowly extending the electronic mechanism and watched as the kitchen moved out. It worked fine. Perhaps in all of this calamity the worst loss would be no wine this night. The bottle which I had unceremoniously deposited in the sink to keep from making a further mess elsewhere now awaited its punishment. Tearstained and dripping I held it up - amazed it hadn't broken and splintered glass all over the floor. There, in sad atonement, the bottle held four inches of its original contents, offering up enough wine for one glass. Miraculously, I think that am one lucky broad; except for the fact that the 30 amp electrical cord didn't reach from this angle, either!

An hour later it was time to handle another

problem with the RV. The hot soapy water in the sink poured out through the bottom panel, covering the linoleum floor and inching toward the carpet. Quick in mopping it up, I could also hear water seeping out the bottom of the RV onto the ground outside my front door. "If it isn't one thing it's your mother!" I cursed under my breath. It was Saturday night and I'd already had a full day of travails, but I decided to continue westward the next day instead of staying put until Monday for two reasons. First, it was not an emergency. The pipes under the kitchen sink had come apart, probably due to a poor fitting job, but even after taking the panel off to assess what had happened under the sink I couldn't see where the problem was. I could wash any dishes that needed to be cleaned at the water faucets supplied in the park grounds or just use the small but effective bathroom sink. Second, I had noticed that there was always RV service in the cities and bigger towns and if I stayed put until Monday because of a place I had seen thirty miles back then I would end up spending what was predicted to be three more days of lousy weather in Kakabecka Falls. That was assuming the place I had passed was authorized to do the work.

The next morning left Kakabecka Falls and

got back on The QEW. The previous day had been long and hard, but there were no tears - except over having only one glass of wine. All of this was teaching me a valuable lesson. When nothing is wrong with the RV be very grateful, for there was always bound to be something lurking around the next corner.

Chapter Four

I'd traveled twenty-three hard hours and had twenty-seven more to go before reaching Banff. Banff had been set as a major destination. When exactly this occurred I don't know but its beauty had been touted and I was eager to spend some time painting there. It had seemed to be so unattainable when I was on the other side of the continent, yet each day I drew a yellow highlighter over the road I had covered and it was inching me a little closer with each tank of gas.

In the end the desire to press forward outweighed resting for a few days to lick my wounds, but I acknowledged the fact that I could not continue to keep this pace.

Every town likes to announce its claim to fame underneath their welcoming sign. One little spot after another would brag of its specialty, together with the population no matter how paltry. I would read them, first with interest and then with some amusement as they began to remind me of Gypsy Rose Lee's song about topless dancing; 'Ya Gotta Have A Gimmick'. *Home To World's Largest Collection of Turkey Taxidermy. Home of Baseball Great Jimmy McCormack. Land Of The Living.* One, however, struck me as downright eye opening. At the bottom of the welcome sign to Raith, Ontario it read, *All waterways from this point north lead to The Artic Ocean.*

I am never without curiosity for the topics I should have paid closer attention to in school. For example, I'd missed Sloth Day altogether. Imagine my shock upon seeing a real live sloth at the Bronx Zoo when I was in my forties. I thought they were extinct ions ago! It seemed the older I got the more interested in the arcane I became. I think most adults are this way. The problem, as I then began to see it, is that school is not for children. They should be playing outside and learning about nature and whatever interests them. We have taken their enthusiasm to learn and squashed it by demanding they accomplish more and more to what end - to get them ready to work. Capitalism - that great machine that churns out humans as its waste bi-product demands its pound of flesh. Education is just the wrong word to use what we are doing to our kids and society should admit it. By the time they reach high school most kids hate learning, especially reading for pleasure. Oh, well, I digress and, once again, my attitudes on this topic would make most people cringe, except of course for the children - they think I am exactly right!

"You can't dance at every party," was what I'd decided as I drove through Kenora. What a magnificent spot, though. One could not wish for more pristine water or pretty coves and panoramic views. Despite the fact that the day was grey and drizzly you couldn't help but feel enveloped in the lushness. A great number of other people thought so, as the city was packed. Boats littered the lakes and restaurants were doing a brisk business. A quick glance at my map gave me confidence to continue to the border. I drove another half hour and then wonder of wonders I had finally exited the great Province of Ontario and entered the Bison Plains of Manitoba, which means Vibrant Energy. Stopping at the information booth had worked so well for me in Ontario I decided it should be my default stop in each of the Provinces. When they told me about a lake that had been made when a meteor hit the earth I was in; boy, a lot of interesting shit happens on this planet!

I called my daughters the next morning from the lovely Provincial Campgrounds, West Hook Lake, eager to share with them both that I was one hour closer to their time zone. My older daughter, Rachael, worked as a consultant in San Francisco, California and lived with her beloved, Andrew. My younger daughter, Leah, was a physical therapist in Scottsdale, Arizona, and lived with her beloved, Rory. Neither had given me grandchildren. I say that not as a statement of fact, but as an accusation, for despite my protestations to the contrary, I think I'd make a damned fine grandma. After long, schmoozy conversations with them both I determined to find a place for the sink's repair. The RV center where I brought The Nest came through with flying colors, identifying a spot in Winnipeg which was only one and a half hours from the crater-formed lake I was at. Their recommendation, Canada One RV, said to could come in that afternoon. Wow! I ran down to the beach so that I could say how beautiful West Hook Lake was. It was.

A quick painless stop in Winnipeg and I was on my way again. It was here a wonderful realization set in; I did not miss my house as much as I loved my new home. This was revealed to me while my nose was in the business of sink-fixing. I found, like other buyers, I had tons more questions that occur only after we have the camper for a while. Maybe that's just me, but I found the more I learned the more frightened I should have been about what I didn't know getting into this proposition in the first place. Like a weeping pressure gauge from the hot water system, or the disappearing black strap from the awning. Or what type of gunk should you use for a sink sealant? Do I really need a level? What will happen to the refrigerator if I don't get one? Why do people have a holder on the ground for their sewer hose? What kind of tape should I use on the extension cover I kinda ripped? O.k. so I forgot to ask that one. As long as they are not looking over their shoulder for the boss, I find RV mechanics an excellent source of information, of good humor and a generally interesting bunch that stay in their field of work forever, or if they leave they always come back, so I've been told.

Greta Garmin let me down. Instead of directing me around Winnipeg she led me straight through the city. It was one of those happy mistakes we sometimes make. What a grand old cosmopolitan center Winnipeg was; so well taken maintained, clean and abound with coordinating flowers. Had this trip been more about being a city mouse than a country mouse I would have found a spot to park and stayed a few days but I had a long stretch of road ahead and Banff was beckoning. Having said that, it was a grueling hour to get through the city and I'm sure many a fellow driver thought I had some nerve taking up so much of the precious asphalt.

I was happy to be back on the open road and, to my wondrous surprise, the great plains of Manitoba were spectacular. I think every hue of green was represented there. There was a green so brilliant it shone like peridot, another green so dull it was closer to grey. There were wheat-tinged greens and purplish blue greens, yellow mustards and flecks of burnt orange green. Fields and layers of greens compounded other greens. I could not wait to try and imitate those colors on my palette! On and on I traveled through the greens until I began to feel like Dorothy in the Wizard of Oz caught in the poppy fields.

It had been a long hard day. Four hours of driving to this point and I'd gone the last forty-five miles looking, without success, for a place to stop. The next Provincial Park was another hundred miles away. Despite good weather I knew I definitely couldn't drive another hour or more, but the thought of going to a private RV campground filled me with dread, for, whether real or imagined, as safe as I felt under the government umbrella was as vulnerable as I felt about something proprietary. Yet, there it was. The ubiquitous brown sign with yellow painting beckoned me. With its

picture of a teepee and something akin to a squarish tin can with wheels I knew it was my cue. *Shady Oaks RV Campground* 3km. That's Canadian talk for less than two miles, so I took a deep breath and got into the left lane in preparation to enter the meridian before crossing over the east bound lane.
As The QEW, forever now known to me as The Great Teat, faded in the distance behind me, I began focusing on the narrow dirt road I had been expected to travel. Not a soul in sight. This is not a good sign. I approached the peeling building, tired and anxious - me not the building - but determined to at least try this venue of camping and promising myself that I always had the option of leaving if it didn't feel right to me. I stopped at the appropriate spot - a sign that said, 'Stop Here'- and got out of The Nest, locking it behind me. The sun was four p.m. strong in the sky, reflecting back my own image in the windows of the little office that also served as a store. It seemed empty. I should leave. No. No, wait. There was a figure waving madly to me behind the counter, I could see him now. He'd spotted me so I opened the door to the sound of little tinkling bells affixed on the jamb to signal potential victims, I mean customers. With what can only be described as a shit-eating grin and eyes that would make Japanese

animee look listless, the Celt put his best brogue forward, "A Grrreat Day, A Fine Day, Eh? How good of ye to come here. Weehhlcome."

"Hello," I responded meekly. I tried to be jovial but his was a tough affect to match.

"What do ye need?" He fairly bellowed the question.

"Well, I'm 32 feet plus another 22 for the car and tow, so I'd like a pull-though."

"Please don't have one please don't have one," I begged silently.

"Noo problem. Will Ye be needin a full hookup?"

I could tell from looking at him that he not only knew the answer to that one but was fully prepared to offer up his complete package, in a manner of speaking.

"That would be fine. How much is it?" Maybe it would be double what I would be willing to pay…

"Well, how long would ye be stayin?" His look shifted now to that of a pound mutt hoping for a new home.

"Just one night."

"Ah… It's $28.00, full hookup, fer the night."

The cheap that is me nodded in agreement, reminding myself, once again, that if at any time I felt uncomfortable I could just leave.

His great toothy grin, undaunted by the

disappointment of a one-nighter, pressed on.
"Tell me, Hooowww did ye find ooouut about our campgrooouuund?"
"Oh, the sign on the road," It seemed obvious.
"Well, we like to knew what's workin and what's not, ye knew."
'Oh, sure," I agreed as the negativity festered persistently. What if I was the only customer he had? What if I was going to be sitting all alone in the middle of a cow pasture somewhere? I could picture myself getting the willies as soon as the sun went down and taking off, bouncing and careening across the field, racing madly back to The QEW; curtains flapping like trashy laundry out the windows and trailing my electric and sewer lines behind me. Forget the water hose - that would have ripped out of the side of the motor home and been left behind like a dead snake at the campground. I could imagine that great smile melting from the cheery faced man at the thought of losing his only customer. I felt guilty for making him so sad and continued to fill out the required paperwork.
"We've got a heated poool!" He bubbled on madly as I wrote.
"Oh, that sounds great," I lied imagining the green slickness of its algae under my feet. Another thought. What if the guy was in a

sex slave trade? What if only lone, unsuspecting travelers like me would come here, so far away from civilization? I tried to make myself feel better, taking consolation in the fact that nobody wanted a 55 year old with tits on her knees. Hey, you never know predilections and such, I retorted defensively, if not weakly, having once heard about a grandma fetish. Next I imagined myself all drugged up on heroine sitting in a corner half naked - wearing nothing but that nice silk robe I've got…

I was shaken from my reverie with the rattling of papers. Here comes the map. There's always a map. It doesn't matter if there are only ten sites, you've got to get the map.

"I've got a super-nice site fer ye," He promised with the enthusiasm of a doctor promising a kid ice cream after the tonsillectomy.

"Terrific!" It was important that I play along, be enthusiastic, at least stay in the moment.

"Lucky number twenty-thhreeee," he said conspiratorially - but still with that great smile and dancing eyes.

Maybe there was something wrong with him. You know how we sometimes overcompensate for a deficiency or a limp or something. I tried to look without looking

but there didn't appear to be anything obvious to the eye. I wandered back to the directions.
"Ye go around and make the second tern, here, see?" The yellow highlighter blazoned the trail for us as if we were on a treasure hunt.
I nodded.
"Then ye go in through this side and yer 'set ups' on the left, see?"
I nodded again, numbly taking the map. "Thank you." I smiled as best I could under the circumstances. I left the office as the little tinkling bell tried, once again, to warn me.

"Mother of God!" I admonished myself, getting into The Nest and starting her up. The heated pool must be inside that shed-like building on the right. Not a chance in hell would I be going in *there.*
Then all of a sudden I see them - bicycles. Lots of bicycles. Children's pink and blue bicycles! I'm going to be o.k., there *are* people here! I'm not alone! I choked back a laughing sob, until, of course, it hit me. This must be a pedophile ring and they are trafficking in children!
That's always my fallback position; if I'm not in trouble then the children must be…
In the distance I see a copse of trees and

there, sprinkled about under the great branch arms are many, many RVs. All different shapes and sizes. Slowly, but at least I'm breathing now, I wind my way into the cool offerings of the shade, checking each orderly branded tree and looking for number 23. As I spot the site and begin to make my most impressive wide turn, out of the corner of my eye I see a flash of a bicycle being frantically pedaled to the front of the site and, who, but the cheeriest man on the planet, springing forth as if thrown off by the bicycle itself. He has come to see that I pull into my cocoon with perfect ease, and that all is working in manner that would make his mother proud. He is waving me in - a little to the right - a little to the left. "Yes, Yes!! That is perfect. You will be so happy and settled here for the night you will wish you could stay for a month!" He seemed to be saying.

I could not stop smiling. I put The Nest in park and sliding open the driver's window ask in almost a giggle of relief, "I forgot to ask your name!"

"It is EWAN," he happily reported. "Ewwwaaahn - my wife, Linda, and I own this park!"

"Thank you, Ewan, Thank you for all your kindness to me this day!"

The cheeriest man on the planet, Ewan, and

I shook hands before he hopped back on his bicycle and scooted back to his post.
For the next few hours as I sipped my rum and coke and happily made what had come to be my favorite dinner, capellini with vegetables, I chortled and snorted heartily, having escaped sure imprisonment and admitting to myself that sometimes a cheery person is just a cheery person and, maybe, just maybe, nothing is wrong with that. George's words, "Fatigue is the great enemy," also rang in my head.

The only thing effective in washing the bugs off the windshield was fresh bug juice. I know that sounds gross, but that was how it felt. Before my eyes bugs as big as small birds arrived at their final destination, to their shock as well as mine. Hordes in every shape and size splattered their most colorful innards on the front of The Nest. By the time I arrived at the information center in Saskatchewan I felt as if I was picking them out of my teeth. The elder balding gentlemen behind the counter eyed me as if they were in my hair as well.
"What can we do for you today." His voice, while not unpleasant, was not the welcome chirping I'd been used to hearing.
"Well, I'm interested in provincial parks that have accommodations for large RV's

pulling a car, not too far off The QEW, as I'm headed for Banff."

A beam from the spot light above made a nice reflective glow above the man's eyebrows. "So, just passing through?" He seemed tired of what was obviously a pretty common low expectation of his fine Province.

"Our parks are pretty far off The QEW." He pulled out a map and made four quick circles, to prove himself correct.

"Oh, well might you recommend some places of interest I would enjoy here?" I'm sorry to say that was rather disingenuous of me, as I really didn't care.

A female volunteer quipped up behind him. "Don't forget to tell her about Moose Jaw!"

He looked back, begrudgingly giving her a nod. "There are lots of nice places to stay in Regina."

I could not believe my ears. Did he say Vagina? "Excuse me?" I asked trying to keep my face from contorting in one direction or another. "Where did you say?"

He said it again, only this time I heard the 'R'.

"I see," I said looking down at the map where he was tapping.

He slid the marker further to my left across The QEW. "Here's Moose Jaw. This has a wonderful tour you wouldn't want to miss."

About an hour's drive past Regina, not Rahgeenah, but Rahjynah, was Moose Jaw. A tour. My interest was somewhat piqued.
"Back in the early 1900's when the Trans Canadian Railroad was built many Chinese were brought into the country to work on the rails. When the work was finished thousands hid in the underground tunnels so that they wouldn't be deported back to China. This tour takes you through the tunnels, showing you were and how they existed. Entire families lived down there. Babies were born and people died. It's really a quite extraordinary bit of history." He looked at me to see if I agreed.
"That *does* sound really interesting," I said gathering momentum, "do you have any literature on that?"
He whipped out the flier faster than you could say 'Chinese immigrant'. He was obviously so pleased to make the sale that it wouldn't be a stretch to imagine that I might have been his first customer ever.
Map and brochure in hand I thanked him for his help and headed back out to the RV.
Ethnocentrism. I may not remember much Mr. Grasso in eleventh grade social studies taught, but I remember that word. It made a huge impression on me - the fact that we believe our culture and ways to be 'right' and every other culture or way to be

'wrong'. It was so obvious, even at a young age. Surely other nations are entitled to live with their rituals and beliefs providing, of course, for human rights. So why, oh tell me why, could I not shake the feeling that naming a city to rhyme with vagina was just *wrong.*

I snickered like an eleven year old, harharing the whole way to Regina. After pulling off The Fair Queen into Buffalo RV Park, finding my site, and turning on the TV I heard that there had been an explosion in Regina. Instead of being concerned I was hysterical laughing at the visualization of it! Was I starting to lose my mind? Too late to ask that question.

*

The first time I invited George to come to my apartment, which reflected a kind of ethereal Carol King album cover, was for dinner and I truly believed it would be the last time I saw him.

"Who is this?" He'd asked grandly upon seeing the little pink stuffed animal sitting happily in the middle of my canopied bed. I had been giving George the nickel tour of the apartment and we'd stopped to linger for the moment in my bedroom.

"Oh, That's Piggie Boi," I'd told him, and then taking my chances I added bravely, "Piggie Boi only knows of love and compassion. He is completely non-judgmental to all. He keeps a journal of our travels together, and I take him with me wherever I go." Piggie Boi was, as always, Calm in the Moment, his little pooch belly protruding past his dirty knees.

"Well, hello, Piggie Boi," George bowed grandly. Piggie Boi was not comfortable with George in the bedroom and so soon after the introduction George was ushered back to the living room. After having made George my best dinner I said goodbye to him assuming that after he'd met Piggie Boi I might have to face the fact that I would not see this man again.

The next day he called me down to his home for a drink.

"I'd like you to meet Rodney," he said to me grandly gesturing to the little stuffed baby gorilla grinning happily at me from the coffee table. "Rodney is a very smart little baby gorilla. He does extra credit reports so that the kids in school get special swim time."

"Well, hello, Rodney!" I picked him up. Rodney, short, squat and cross-eyed, sported a Christmas stocking cap with a little pin of a dagger dripping blood that he had obviously gotten from daddy. Like Piggie Boi, Rodney seemed to share an aversion to bath time.

“Hoo Hoo Hoo!” said Rodney.

“He’s very excited to meet you,” said George.

“And I am very excited to meet him!”

George and I were mates.

We shared a wondrous joy of extreme creativity; our family growing in leaps and bounds. Children were coming from all corners of the world to be with us. Patty Platypus swam from New Zealand to join George on the Hudson River. Gordon was a runaway gargoyle from Notre Dame, coming to me because he was frightened that he was going to be turned into a Ken doll. Manny and Danny, the mandrill twins, were the athletes, practicing day and night for a spot in the circus. We had room for a cranky, one-legged female Santa named Sandy, and Cubby, a cross dresser, who was always trying on my earrings. Murdock, George’s secretary and a heck of a vulture, looked after the kids when we went out and perched happily on top of our eight foot cactus which doubled as a Christmas tree in season. We took the kids with us to watch my daughter, Leah, play university volleyball, setting them up on the bleachers in front of us. She was not amused. We took them on book signings, where they took turns holding the pen for daddy. They had their pictures taken on safari in South

Africa, at Ariau Jungle in the Amazon, in the L'Hotel Sainte Germaine in Paris, and at the Wailing Wall in China. We took them wherever we went as good will ambassadors and they thrived on the exposure. Despite all of their plans for what they might be when they grew up we knew, of course, that they would never grow old or leave us.

*

Laundry Time. The laundry room was a pleasant surprise, clean and new, but I needed loonies and toonies. A loonie is a one dollar coin, a toonie speaks to deductive reasoning. The woman behind the counter at the office was happy to exchange bills for the loonietoones and we got to talking. Sharon and her daughter, Cheryl, ran the park but the great love of their lives was to breed and show Scottie dogs. We spoke at length about her love of the breed until her daughter came into the office from having shown a camper where their site was.

"Cheryl," the mother called her attention to our conversation. "We're talking about the Scotties."

Cheryl turned happily to me, eager to speak with anyone interested in her passion.

"I used to have Maltese." I said remembering the experience fondly. "She was bred and had five beautiful little boys!" I removed a picture of the pure white puppies against the background of a red tablecloth from my wallet to show them.

We had gotten the dogs because my girls, 'tweens at the time, had begged and pleaded for them; including presenting my husband with a signed contract solidifying their absolute intent to take care of all of the dog's needs. Mind you, I said 'intent'... We enjoyed Vanilla Wafer immensely, despite the fact that on rainy cold nights it was the girls' poor father out in the misery holding the pink leash and an umbrella over them both. We wanted Wafer to enjoy all of the aspects of as full a life as we could provide and for some ridiculous reason we thought this had to include motherhood. Remembering well the day we dropped her off at the breeder with her little pink hair bow perched perkily atop her head and her school bag placed on the chair beside us, the breeder offered for us to see her mate - warning us to hold Wafer tightly for the little breeder would try to 'take a shot' as she put it, from where he sat. She bragged a bit about his lineage and although Wafer's teeth were a little undershot she agreed to breed her. We pleaded her case by saying she had a fine temperament. Sheesh; my husband and I didn't have to go through such machinations to breed! Fortunately all went well and we kept one of the little "mookie boys," as they had come to be known. So, to say I had bred Maltese was a bit of a stretch of the truth, but still the experience did qualify the statement in general conversation.

"You know, after we have bred the dogs and they have gone as far as they can go in show we try to find happy homes for them."

"Really?" I responded with interest.

"My husband and I took in Labradors from the rescue squad when we lived on the Hudson. It was a perfect spot for them since we were always home there were no children and they could go swimming eight months of the year."

She looked at me thoughtfully before proceeding. "I have a wonderful five year old female named Pumpkin Pie that I would love to find a good home for. Do you think you would like to meet her?"

So many people travel with their animals. It might be good company for me. It might even be considered a safety issue.

"I'd love to," I said.

*

"Is it too soon to talk about keeping him?" George had hesitated before asking the question, daring not to hope.

I started laughing. It was that nervous kind of laugh where you already know the outcome of the situation. "Well, if no one claims him then I don't see why not, but it's a beautiful dog, George, surely someone must be missing him by now." I put the plastic container of chopped meat, just cooked and cooled, on the ground. The black lab gobbled it up hungrily. "Looks like he hasn't eaten in a while. I'll call the town animal controller and see if anyone is missing their dog."

The animal controller had been on a drinking toot for three days - nobody knew where he was. I called the local animal hospital. They had no listing for the lab but suggested we bring him in, which we did.

What a shock it was to learn that the poor dog was in third stage heart worm and that arsenic was the only remedy. We both cried to think of how frightened he'd been when someone dumped the poor thing off The New York State Thruway, which the vet said happened pretty regularly. We resolved to take care of the dog, whether it lived through the dosages or not.

A few years back George had won an award from Ellery Queen with a short story entitled, *The Problem With the Pig*. We always wanted a big fat pink pig for a pet because we'd heard they were very smart and clean. Living in Nyack on the second floor made it no more than a dream, but here in our own house we were free to have that pig and all the kids had been eagerly awaiting its arrival. This majestic, sphinx-like pitch black English Lab showed up first, so we named him Pig.

Then we got a Yellow Lab, Biff, to keep Pig company. Then we got another rescue Lab, Dakota, to keep Biff company. Then Leah's cat had kittens and I took a female, Miss Rheingold, to keep me company.

"I'm ashamed to tell you this, Robin, but other than you I love these dogs more than anything or anyone in the whole wide world!"

"Don't worry, George," I comforted him and told him a truth he could not have suspected. Most everyone feels that way about their animals."

*

Cheryl came by The Nest about eight at night with Pumpkin Pie. I was immediately struck by how calm and docile the Scottie was. Her jet black hair had been kept long and was meticulously tended to. I put out my hand for her to sniff me and, unafraid, she came over to do so. Now that she was closer I could see that her eyes, underneath those long eyebrows, were equally dark and her nose didn't have the slightest imperfection. Ears high in the fore and tail sweeping up in the aft, I was certain she showed well.

"She has a bit of red in her," Cheryl offered as proof that Pumpkin Pie would never win in show.

"Cheryl, she's beautiful," I said, now stroking her soft hair.

The most unusual feature for me to get used to about PP was her long snout. It seemed to be half the size of her body and, after the Labs and Maltese, I found it a little unsettling. A paltry thought and not like me to look a gift horse in the mouth, so to speak, I was a little disappointed in myself.

"I have to get back out to the office to check in late comers, why don't you keep her with you for a while?"

"O.k." I said, almost childlike.

After Cheryl left I talked to PP for a while. She was polite but noncommittal. I picked her up and put her on my bed. She seemed very content to be pet and scritchelled. I took a picture of her with my cell phone and emailed it to the girls with the message "What do you think?" Both offered the same sensible advice I would have given them. "It doesn't matter what *we* think, what matters is what *you* think." Thanks for nothing.

I started to think about the winter just passed and, despite the comfort of this sweet creature, I became sadder and more confused. Pig had died of sclerosis of the liver four years after we got him, probably from the arsenic given to treat his heartworm. George had been absolutely despondent for months afterwards. Biff, while mourning the loss of his mentor and good buddy, carried on better than George and became the head honcho, except of course, for the cat. After George died Biff and Dakota became as messy as I'd been. It was a sad, sad life for the dogs and, although I had cried in anguish, apologizing profusely to George for not keeping them with me, the minute I had them placed in happy homes I knew it was the right decision. Biff went to a family with teenage boys; a situation that would have been disastrous for him just a few years earlier, and Dakota went to a loving home with lots of property as a pet for a teenage girl, also something that would not have been possible without all of the love and patience George had showered upon them both. He would have been so proud to know they were ready to live with others without fears and anxieties. The cat was another matter. The most emotion she had shown through all of this Strum and Drang was to honor me with her presence by climbing into bed with me at night for about ten minutes before going back downstairs. I, however, loved that cat out of all proportion to what she could possibly give me back. She was mostly an outdoor cat, still hunted, and came into 'the barn' only when it got too cold for her outside. How many nights I had carried on and wrung my hands because it was pitch black out and she would not (or could not!) come inside. George admitted that he didn't love her but that he found her interesting.

It was also not lost on me when a good friend of the family and therapist had said, "Robin, you have been taking care of George for a long time and now you worry about Missy running out of the camper at her first opportunity and what would happen to her. Worrying will become a part of your life and it will cripple you."

Letting go of Miss Rheingold was excruciating but it was in her best interest so I did it, hysterically crying as I drove the whole way to her new home. She didn't even say goodbye. I realized very quickly that each time I cried thinking of Missy within five minutes I was crying for George.

Sadly, I picked up Pumpkin Pie and escorted her to back the office.

"I'm sorry Cheryl, she is absolutely wonderful, but I can't do it."

"I know," she acknowledged, "Timing is everything and it's just too soon for you."

Nodding in agreement and surprised I didn't

feel worse about the decision I knew in my heart that I just could not bear another loss.

Chapter Five

Someone should tell the information center not to recommend places RV's can't get to. There was no place, I mean n-o p-l-a-c-e for me to park in Moose Jaw so I had to press on. I landed in Swift Current which was being over run with rats, as the local news station reported it. I was so fucking miserable; pushing too hard, eating too much, drinking too much. I couldn't stand myself. I threw up. When will I stop pushing like this?

The winds were howling outside and the RV rocked back and forth. I retracted the extensions and the smell of vomit made me sicker. As I watched TV and listened to the symptoms for ovarian cancer I was certain I had it. I was kidding myself by pretending I had a sensitive stomach and that the water was bad, or that perhaps the frying pan I'd been cooking in had high levels of iron, or maybe that the local fruit was poisoned with pesticides. It might be the H1N1 virus. Also, all those years of keeping kosher was *nothing* compared to the amount of effort and time I was putting in on sanitation, keeping my hoses and connectors in separate compartments underneath the chaise was like keeping the meat away from the dairy -

all I needed was one rogue bug to do me in. Maybe parts of my RV were made with poisonous materials from overseas! Maybe it's something else I wasn't even aware of, but every single day there was something else physically wrong with me. I was convinced I was dying.

There was a squeaking noise coming from the bedroom and so I went back to investigate. Against the window, over a framed picture of George and me in front of The Louvre taken twelve years ago was a fir branch scratching against the pane. Like an elongated hairy finger it scritcheled softly but insistently. George wants me to hold him again. If I do will I feel better? Will he feel better? Will it keep him alive?

*

San Bernardo Island off the coast of Brazil was a paradise. We laid complacently across the hump of the mastiff-like rock with a towel over our faces to shade us from the brilliant summer sun of February.

"I'll be lovin' you always." The smell of his breath laced with rum punch and faint Marlboro soothed my soul as if it were fresh lavender.

"I'll be lovin' *you* always."

We had recited the singsong line to each other in the comings and goings of our days for two years now. The 'goings' had become less and less, however, since I stopped managing a software training center and focused on becoming a potter full time. George could not have been happier having me with him all day long, every day, and, as glorious as the days had been living together sailing our 16 foot Hobbie catamaran in the summer and keeping warm through the harsh winters enveloped in each other's arms, when an opportunity to travel abroad presented itself we'd jump at the chance.

He stirred from his sleepy frame, speaking in earnest. "Before we found each other I was content. If I had died, Robin, I would have been satisfied leaving the opus of my life's work. I never expected the gift of you. I never expected all of the gifts that have come to me through you."

George had become more comfortable leaving The Yacht Club, as we called our home on The Hudson in Nyack. His great love for music and my willingness to drive was enough encouragement to get him into Manhattan for operas. As long as I was his 'wrangler', he was willing to accept an invitation to go to France to promote his works, and even more impressively, I'd gotten him to accompany me to visit both his and my family in what were lovingly referred to as 'command performances.' Also, I'd started a small publishing company to make his out of print works available through the new print on demand technology and he'd accepted a few invitations for book signings - deliciously shocked to learn that his audience was now including college-aged readers with multicolored hair and body piercings. Having said I was 'the wheels' of the operation, George was introducing me to a world I barely knew existed. I'd never studied great music, traveled extensively, or explored other cultures.

"Before we met I would have been satisfied and content with life, my George. Now you can see I'm hungry to live. Suffice to say we have brought each other great gifts."

"This very *moment* of love is our eternity," he'd said stroking my hair.

*

One good thing about moving through topographical areas without a time sensitive goal is that if the weather gets lousy you can just pick up and go. Another two hours away it will probably be better. That thought helped me move through the wind and rain and ennui so that I could leave Swift Current. Once again I promised to take it easy and this time I kept that promise by driving only three hours, which brought me into the Province of Alberta and The

Tillebrook Provincial Park.

Unfortunately that good idea was not manifested; the weather in Alberta was no better. Having no idea how nice or ugly the park I was in was I kept my snout to the ground, setting up the only amenity afforded, a 20 amp connection before hustling back inside The Nest. I put on my thermals and some hot music to dance to, in the hopes it would raise my spirits and my body heat. It did little for the first but a satisfactory job on the second.

I pulled out the big map and tried to take comfort in how long the yellow highlighted line was. I'd come so far! Fourteen more driving hours to Vancouver, that wasn't bad. There was actually light at the end of the continent. Five more hours to Calgary. My nerves were shot. If I can just get to Banff I will stop racing like a mad woman.

I permitted my mind to wander further down the road and into the future. In two and a half weeks I would be meeting my sister, Mimi, at the airport in Seattle where she would be flying in from New York and since arrangements needed to be made I focused my efforts on where to stay, especially since it would be Labor Day weekend and, unlike the Great Civic Weekend of Canada, I knew exactly what I'd be in for. I called the Washington State Parks reservation number but the woman on the other end had no idea where the airport was in relation to the parks that permitted RVs. I looked at the map closer, hoping a little airplane would appear somewhere amidst all the water and shoreline that is Seattle, but nothing had landed since the last time I'd looked so, in guesstimate, I chose Kananstat State Park in Enumclaw. Then I made arrangements for a campground in the Willamet Valley wine area of Oregon as well as Jedidiah State Park in the redwood forests of California. In Calistoga I threw a dart at the map as I had for Seattle, hoping the campground would be close to the mud baths and wineries. A good piece of right brained work completed, I felt I had accomplished something which justified laying about for the rest of the day. When I woke at six a.m. I could hear the heavy rain. It was beating me down - another miserable day. And freezing! I'd worn two sets of thermals to bed. Depressed, I pulled the covers over my head. An hour later I was woken by two women walking and talking. The rain must have stopped if only for a few moments. I fell back asleep. At eight I got up and slogged about outside, miserably, to close up and face the day. I threw Clorox into the fresh water tank and, not having unhitched Maxine, drove all 52 feet that was me to the dump station where I emptied the grey and black tanks before letting the water run out of the fresh water tank and refilling it; just in case I'd have to stay at the next campground 'dry' - without any amenities. When I attempted to wash out the sewer hose with the unpotable water the force was so strong that it splashed water up into my face, hair and sweats. Cursing, I climbed back into The Nest, put Clorox water on a washcloth and proceeded to wash my face with the cold water before changing my clothes and slicking my hair back. Looking in the mirror and saw myself tired and disgusted and, feeling that I just couldn't be any more miserable, I raised my hands and face to the heavens, shouting the immortal words of Captain Kirk, "Beam Me Up, Scottie!!!"

The drive into Calgary was uneventful, aside from putting eye drops in every ten minutes to staff off a possible eye infection, but the drive from Calgary to Banff was spectacular as you could see the great mountains rise from the flatness like giants. I'd made it! I felt so insignificant driving through the pass into Banff National Park and yet absolutely exhilarated at the same time, giddy with anticipation for the great weather they had been experiencing and a chance to stay in one place long enough to get into a rhythm

of painting.
"Yes." They had room for me.
"Yes." I will become a member.
How long will I be staying? I decided on the spot. A week. Do you have a week available?
Yes, again. A full week of yesses in front of me, I proceeded into the park and up to Tunnel Mountain where I would be staying.
Full hookup but no pull through, I disconnected Maxine and backed into spot 150. My 'neighbor' would also back in so that our rears would face each other, bumpus to bumpus so to speak. The length of the RVs ran parallel to the road. I could feel the horrors of the previous days blow off me into the afternoon winds and out to the mountains' peaks. Within the hour I had showered and had even taken out a canvas folding chair to set outside my door, like a real person who is going to stay for a while would.
Actually, real campers do a hell of a lot more than that! I'd seen the usual lanterns and ground ornaments but I was really tickled the day I saw a water fountain in the 'front yard.' Now *that's* setting up camp!
Donning shorts and sneakers for the first time in weeks, I put my whistle around my neck and headed out to walk on one of the hundreds of hiking trails throughout the

great park. At a lookout point I saw a couple walking their tiny dog. They looked to be of retirement age and without a whiff of perversion so I approached them with a broad smile.

"Do you mind if I join you?" I asked, hoping they might find me whiff less, as well. And then as by way of explanation, added, "I'm traveling alone and don't think I should hike by myself."

"Sure!" the man lit up instantly, obviously happy for the opportunity to meet someone new. "I'm Wilf and this is my wife, Arlene."

She smiled her acceptance of me kindly.

As we fell into step I couldn't help but notice that the tiny pup was keeping up by what amounted for it as running. "I notice a lot of people travel with dogs. How does your little one like it?"

"Oh, Pixie? She's happy as long as she's with Arlene. When we got her from the pound she was afraid of everything…"

"He's always down there looking at the dogs," she added shyly.

"Yeah, well, so many need homes." His happy countenance took a temporary downturn.

"My husband and I took in labs on The Hudson River in New York." I let them know I was a dog lover, too.

The easy conversation turned quickly. Wilf was obviously passionate about his politics. "What do you think is going to happen with the healthcare system in America?"
I was actually surprised to hear him use the word America to describe The United States of America, since Canada and Mexico are America, too. "It will be interesting," I said noncommittally. I was not interested in hiking the two miles in solitude or, worse, angry abject silence with near strangers. I turned the question. "How do you feel about the system you have here in Canada?"
"Well," he started thoughtfully. "Despite what you might hear in The States, we actually are very satisfied. It's true you might have to wait for testing for something that's not a crisis, but if it's an emergency you get all the testing and attention you need immediately."
Arlene chimed in. "Like when my knee hurt and I didn't want to wait six weeks to have an MRI done I just paid the $300.00 to have it taken care of right away."
"Yeah, so it's not a perfect system, but it works and we are always trying to make it better."
Having been both schooled in and taught university ethics, I had come to the conclusion that objectivity on a political position was an oxymoron. An individual's

strong emotional feelings were basely, if not cognitively, reflected in their political views. Never had I witnessed a purely logical discussion, but rather great logic skills, like those of William F. Buckley, that served the emotional neediness of the person pleading acceptance of their view, either the right or left leanings. The fact that the positions might be pleaded with an unemotional affect simply speaks to an individual's desire to appear logical, like a Mr. Spock. The expression 'figures lie and liars figure' amuses me greatly. This is not to say that new information isn't welcoming, but in presenting Supreme Court Opinions to students for parsing I had never come across a student who changed their position on an issue; rather they had merely been given more ammunition to support their own fears, hopes or neediness. It would seem to follow that the less you cared the more rational you could be. Yes. The individual who can say, "I don't have an opinion on that topic," might be 'logically persuaded' by appealing to some need within themselves. This is why politicians can be great orators - they are, generally speaking, emotionally needy individuals but quick witted.

Wilf and Arlene's remarks were ones of pride in belonging to a culture that believed in providing for all its members, at least giving it their best effort. George would have loved that. In The United States we would refer to Wilf and Arlene as socialists. To us this word has a bad connotation, reminiscent of The Cold War Era, but since the 1930's we have, in fact become more social concerned. I'm always surprised at conservative individuals who oppose a national health care system but who are extremely grateful for Medicare for their parents, or Social Security benefits, or the public school system. Everybody has an emotional 'button'.

Pixie, Arlene, Wilf and I stopped at a view point to take in the magnificence of Bow River and hoodoos. The hoodoos reminded me of when we were kids and would drip wet sand through our fist to see how high of a pile we could make. They were a succession of water and wind eroded rocks, cream colored and softened by time. The Bow River wound lazily about below us, its emerald green water a reminder that you would die of hypothermia before drowning. I watched some teenagers crawling up the hoodoos like so many ants trying to see how high they could climb before slipping back down. I couldn't decide whether I thought they were crazy to take such chances or if I was just jealous. That's what happens when you get older…

My attention turned back to Wilf who had started a conversation with a rather dapper, older gentleman on the point. Within thirty seconds of finding out the man was from Salt Lake City, Utah, Wilf had asked if he was a Mormon, the man had admitted he'd fallen from the fold and married a Roman Catholic, Wilf had asked if he had more wives, the man had replied that he didn't nor did Mormon's believe in that anymore, Wilf had brought up an HBO show about present day polygamy, and in final retaliation, the white-haired gentleman blew back that with all the same sex marriages in San Francisco it's a wonder the whole country is going to hell in a hand basket! Emotional buttons abound…

Despite the fact that Arlene was standing about rather sheepishly I enjoyed the exchange. Wilf was obviously uninhibited in both vantage point and expression. While others might consider his frankness past the parameters of appropriateness I liked his openness. You would certainly know how he felt on any given topic; any lean towards caginess seemed out of the question. He was probably a lousy poker player.

We walked on with Pixie in the lead.

More gentile to social amenity, Arlene spoke of family. "We're going to see my son and his wife in Calgary tonight for dinner."

"How lovely! Is he your only child?" I'm not sure about my own social skills, but once the die is cast I'm in.

"No. We have four - two are fostered. My brother is coming into Calgary with his wife, too, which is why we came down from Edmonton to stay in Banff for a few days and have a nice family visit tonight."

"That's pretty far." I was calculating an hour or so of driving each way.

"Well, we might stay over but they have two cats and I'm not sure Pixie is going to be alright with them."

"Wouldn't she be happier staying in your camper?"

"No Way!" Wolf quipped. "She gets very upset to be left alone. If we have to come back tonight then we will - I just won't drink."

It didn't take me long to volunteer. "I'll be happy to watch her for the night. Why don't you come to my RV for a glass of water after our walk and see how she does. It would certainly make it easier for you."

They were obviously pleased with the offer but skeptical.

Hey, maybe I'd found a niche for myself - traveling dog watcher.

It felt kinda nice...

After they had a nickel tour of The Nest,

Arlene and Pixie sat on the couch. Wilf chose the captain's chair that swiveled around to face the living area. I sat at the kitchen table, coaxing Pixie. "Yes, Girl, you like it here, don't you?" We laughed.

"This is awfully nice." Wilf looked around the room, nodding his head in approval.

"Thanks, Wilf, but what does Pixie think?"

Pixie obviously did not think much, her brown eyes and pink nose fixed squarely on Arlene. I rose to get us glasses of water and gave her some in a little dish which she gladly lapped up. We chatted on amiably for a while longer before the verdict came in.

"I think we'll take her with us tonight, Wilf," Arlene pled the case. "You know how nervous she gets when I'm gone."

"True enough. She might pee or get crazy and then you'd be stuck, Robin."

I nodded my head in understanding. "Let me know if you change your mind any other time - I'll be around for a week."

"Us, too," Arlene said. "We're in site 208. Come by and see us."

As they rose to leave the camper I assured them I would stop by sometime within the next few days.

A very pleasant exchange except for the fact that George had had nothing to add to the conversation, which is so unlike him.

When they left I got out the Spot Shot.

Pixie had peed on my couch, probably just from having the thought that they might leave her…

I was surprised to see Wilf and Arlene pull up alongside The Nest about two hours later. I went outside as Wilf rolled down his window and rested his crooked arm on the ledge, sticking his head out. "Do you want to come to our campsite for dinner tomorrow? We're having bison steak."

"Sure!" I responded enthusiastically. "I'll bring the focaccia bread and a salad."

"Make it Fiveish, I make a mean gin and tonic."

"I'll be there. Thanks, guys. Have a great evening in Calgary."

As we waved our goodbyes I took an appreciative look at the sun's shadows playing tag amidst the mountains and valleys and decided the time was right to try to express three dimensions on a two dimensional medium. I chose a canvas and set up my easel and paints.

The only passage of time I felt was my frantic race against the setting sun as I hurried to capture the final strains of a color washed scene. Compared with so many recent evenings, it was actually a joy to finally not have enough time in the day, as opposed to slogging through several long, seemingly motionless nights.

I'd been up a few times during the night - plagued by a fluttering and frightened moth which must surely have had a three foot wing span. I couldn't imagine how it had gotten into the camper. Perhaps it was the air conditioning unit? If there is a duct big enough for something that size to get through what would prevent locusts or tsetse flies?? The fact that neither were indigenous to the area did not help to assuage my fears. While I was up I contemplated what I would do if I did, indeed, get a heart attack.

Despite the fitful sleep I woke the next morning cold but happy. I bemoaned having to go outside to turn on the propane so I could turn on the heat inside but it turned out to be a blessing as the rising sun shone magnificently on the face of Banff Mountain. As if it weren't spectacular enough, the morning sun was like a spot light that said to all of Banff, "Look At Me! Look At Me!" I was certainly in no hurry to go back inside now, realizing that The Nest was actually colder than the campground. After enjoying the view for a few moments longer I made coffee, warmed up and turned on the television to see what the weather report for the day would be. They were expecting a breezy 20 degrees Celsius - maybe that's about 65 degrees in Yankee talk (Fahrenheit). Since there was now a two hour time difference between New York and Alberta, I touched base with a few of my beloveds back East who I had committed to calling with some regularity before climbing into Maxine and heading out to The Hot Springs. It was the first time I'd driven the car in quite a while and so at first it felt as if something were wrong. I was *way* too close to the ground, certain I would need to use my feet like Fred Flintstone to make the tiny car go forward. Additionally, I kept checking the speed, as it seemed as if I was wildly careening when in actually I was well within the speed limit. What a huge difference navigating The Nest had made in my driving perception!

Within five minutes I had entered the fairyland that is Banff. The meticulously clean little village with it's coordinated storefronts nestled perfectly in a vale. I imagined the zoning board to be rigid in its demand for conformity and am not always impressed when they are successful, as some 'planned' areas seem to be contrived and without character. Such was not the case with Banff. It was delightful and, while I am not a shopper, I can appreciate a town with a wide main street, plenty of parking and a variety of little shops. I proceeded onto a bridge over The Bow River before heading up a steep incline to The Hot Springs. Once there the gatekeeper advised me that the hot springs were tepid today, so he gave me a dollar off the $7.50 entrance fee. Sheessh. Even at 36 degrees it was delicious to sit on a ledge in the great tiled pool and have one of the pressure faucets aimed at my lower back. Within a half of an hour the Lombard twinge had dissipated.

I had read wonderful things about the scenic views one could enjoy from the crest of Banff Mountain by taking the gondola ride to the top so I paid the usual overpriced tourist fee and waited patiently to be ushered into the little glass capsule. With two young girls who did not speak English, I bobbed precariously up the slopes for the next ten minutes, enjoying the vista, especially looking down upon a castle-like edifice, The Banff Springs Hotel. As I reached into my pocketbook to take out my camera I noticed for the first time that I had left my wedding ring on the bedroom end table. I became very upset as a lump came into my throat. "Don't you dare cry," I was fierce in my determination to remain even keeled. "It happens. Live with it."

While I had told myself that I wore the ring because I didn't want to encourage any male overtures, another, obviously more important reason was because I still felt married to George and didn't want to go anywhere without him. For the first time it struck me that I had been wearing the ring as a prop. I became very angry at this thought, but it could not be denied. I had been wearing that ring for twelve years now. Keeping predators at bay? Keeping me married to my George? Or 'prop'. How dare I! I am disgusted with myself and so on went the battle of my disloyalty to George in my head.

For the rest of the morning I was acutely aware of feeling lonely. Why did it matter so much? It was not as if I was reflecting on how much we would have loved sharing the experience of Banff together, because George wouldn't have enjoyed it, and maybe that was the problem. Even if I could have encouraged him to leave The Compound, he had been so sick the last two years he would have been hard pressed to walk the short distance from the parking lot to the gondola. Maybe I felt guilty going on without him. No matter whatever else had happened since he died, I had never minded being alone before that moment but now I had thought, "How good it would be to have someone to talk to." In what I later realized was exactly nine months to the day since George died, it was the first time I ever felt an ache for someone's company.

By the time I returned back to The Nest the feeling had subsided, for I felt at peace in my home and away from others, no longer confronted with my aloneness. I was content, once again, to open my palette case and smell the delicious scent of oils before choosing a new canvas. Time again passed quickly and the afternoon breezes had picked up their pace, letting me know that if I wanted to fit in a walk before dinner I'd better get moving.

Hooking up with Arlene and Wilf had proved to be such a fine experience I decided to continue the practice, happy in my determination to be outdoors more and exercising regularly. Whistle and keys around my neck and wedding band firmly on my finger I proceeded to the lookout point, directly across the street from The Nest, and waited patiently for a hiking couple to come by. My wait was short lived. Herman, an engineer for Lockheed Martin, and Sonia, a school teacher, were a retired couple that lived in Duluth, Michigan. They enjoyed coming over the border into Canada regularly for their summer vacations. It seemed perfect. They were happy to have me join them and, while they were a little more ambitious in physical exertion than Arlene and Wilf, I was determined to keep up. Somewhere between conversation about Herman's work in a government security facility and my discussion of George's espionage novels the political views of Herman and Sonia surfaced. They stated President Obama was an arrogant black man (who did not know his place?) akin to Hitler, and George W. Bush had been a brilliant president. They saw no conflict in ideology between the socialization of our education system, the Medicare both sets of their parents received, the social security benefits they retired on and their stance on a national health care plan, which they were adamantly against.

Surely there is room for all ideologies in moderation, as the capitalist health program would still be available to all who were more comfortable with it? I had suggested without vehemence.

Even this concept was unacceptable. It was more than unacceptable it was, in the true sense of the word, unfathomable. Their racism, hates and mostly fears were so deeply ingrained that there was no room for them to even entertain other possibilities. Money for war against Iraq? Yes, they understood the necessity of giving that burden to their children. Money for the 'waste product' of our capitalist machine - our fellow citizens? No.

They believed that God, indeed, blessed

their America and did *not* believe that other nations should find their car bumper sticker to that effect frightening or threatening, but they also believed that a bumper sticker which said Allah Protect Arabs was, indeed, a frightening and threatening statement that could not be tolerated. Sonia and Herman could find no conflict in holding these two completely opposite views as absolute truths. Insisting we were a Christian Nation because our money said, "In God We Trust" and that the pledge of allegiance contained "Under God", they were unable to integrate the fact that both of those acts were unconstitutional, having been instituted in the 1950's during The McCarthy Era and no one I know of, present day, would consider that period of history one of our shining moments. Specific to our constitution there was *never* to be mention of *any* god in government, lest one view of 'ism' be shown favor over another. This fact was clearly in the way of their view.

George used to say that evil was a lack of compassion. I thought, "These people look pretty on the outside, but they are emotionally-deformed inside."

Not altogether disingenuously I thanked Herman and Sonia for letting me join them on their walk and hurried back to The Nest to prepare my contribution for dinner with

Arlene and Wilf. The conversation with them over drinks and a meal would be most stimulating. Having had so much hateful heat blown at me that afternoon and retaliated, if only in my heart against their darkness, I thought, once again, how we *all* use our wonderful logic skills to service our emotions!

*

Part of the new millennium celebration for The Gannett Newspaper would be an article by George C. Chesbro on his hopes and dreams for the future of mankind. On January 2, 2009 George took his case to the public for the first time in a non-fiction form. Even if you abhorred his view you still had to admire his courage. I, personally, was frightened what the backlash would bring. It had taken him only one afternoon to write a full newspaper page on what he referred to as growing up and letting go of magical thinking. A recurring theme in most of his works, George felt very strongly that in order for the species to survive we would have to overcome one of our biggest, possibly genetic, obstacles; the belief in Santa Claus for adults - god. And that anyone who was a card carrying member of such an organization was intellectually diminished, not only by being submissive to six silly things before breakfast but by experiencing a lack of appreciation for and diminishment of this wonderful life experience of sentience because they believed they had lives *before* this one and/or lives *after* this one. He pled against divisiveness, he pled for accepting responsibility for our actions without using terms like 'evil' and 'good' and to use mental health as the goal of acting in our best interests. He pled to let history speak for itself - Hammurabi constructing the social ethical system a thousand years before religions picked it up as their own. He tried to point out the illogic of a statement like, "God saved my little girl from the burning building." o.k. - so the other little girl who was not saved by God…? Or the athlete who had won in competition praising the Lord - God wanted your opponent to lose? Was your opponent 'bad' and you are 'good'? George hoped that people would question everything they had been taught and take the time to look carefully into the veracity of statements they had grown up believing. It was not that he did not acknowledge the mysteries of the universe, he reveled in all seen and unseen, but that did *not* mean causation. If we don't know how something works so, then, we don't know - but don't make something up to make yourself feel better - just acknowledge that you don't know. Maybe in time we will understand more of how life works, and maybe we won't, but either way that doesn't mean there is Some *thing* benevolent or malevolent making it happen. More often it's some *one* or some *institution* making it happen.

Although we received many phone calls from people who appreciated George's view, the mail delivered only one letter from a minister pleading his case for religion as an ethical based system.

In *Affair of Sorcerers* George's storytelling had taken one of his favorite mystery characters, Dr. Robert Frederickson on a journey through many ideologies and while Mongo, as he was known to friends, lived in the real world there were those truly suffering from what they *believed* was happening because of their magical thinking predilections. A novel always in option for movie, I was most sorry George did not live to see that particular story come to the big screen, for although it was written over thirty years ago it is as fresh today as the day he conceptualized the plot.

In some universities George's works are studied under the headings of 'critical thinking skills' and 'tech noir". *Candala*, a story about the Indian caste system, followed the deterioration of a man who believed himself to be from a high caste. When he found out the opposite to be true he imploded with devastating results; all because he was a card carrying member of a system, not an individual able to identify himself without belonging to it.

Although George chortled heartily at the fact that he was never able to answer the questions put to the students at the end of his own short stories - especially ones that opened with "What was the author thinking…" because George was never quite sure what he was thinking - one question he could always answer. The moral of the story is 'be very careful about what you believe in, for that belief will subordinate you.'

*

I had completely trashed my little kitchen in an attempt to make focaccia bread, a feat that had been easily accomplished hundreds of times before in a standard kitchen was a disaster here. Flour and chopped veggies were all over the floor as I searched in vain for one more counter top to place ingredients on. Setting the little oven at 400 degrees had singed the bottom of the bread so badly that I had to surgically remove the burnt to salvage something of the offering I had committed to. Trying to make a spinach salad at the same time was a comedy of errors. Hard boiled eggs - not happening. What the heck had I done with that honey mustard? My kingdom for a splatter grate to put over the bacon!

Never late for cocktails in my life, I arrived at Campsite 208 ten minutes late. Of course when you are camping 'late' is a silly concept, and it was especially so with Arlene and Wilf, who looked as if they would be expecting company in about an hour *after* I arrived. Following a great Japanese rule to make no excuses, I presented the bread and salad graciously, giving no exasperated story. Fortunately the taste had not suffered and none were the wiser of my experience. Next time I would do better.

Arlene and Wilf were a delicious blend of anecdotal stories and interesting arcane factoids about Canada. I learned that there are over one thousand glaciers in Banff and that every spring Fenland Trail is closed for the elk calving. Tunnel Mountain, where we were staying, was over fifty-five hundred feet high and they said that I should very well expect to see wolves, bears, and elk in the park. After I shared my silliness about passing through Regina (in a manner of speaking) they advised me, straight faced of course, that Regina means Regent or Queen.

I guess that little tidbit fell somewhere between anecdotal story and interesting factoid. While they were very proud of their Province and their country they didn't hesitate to share with me facts that disturbed them. Over forty percent of Albertans did not vote they had sadly admitted, and they had the lowest rate of donor organs in Canada. This troubled them terribly - as it would any socially conscious individual.
With Wilf in four curling leagues, they had no intention of leaving Edmonton in the winter, and both absolutely relished the cold. They planned on traveling to The Yukon next spring - maybe I would like to go, too?
The bison steak tasted like lean cow and I could not imagine that it would disturb my stomach. All seemed right with the world.

Chapter Six

The next morning I woke to find an e-mail from Mel, George's agent with The William Morris Agency in New York. Contractual arrangements for an option had been agreed upon for *Bone,* a best seller in France which had been in option several times before without making it to the screen. It is considered by many to be his best work, but his cult fans in the United States would disagree. How funny it had been to George to see young people with nose rings and spiky colored hair gush over Beasts of Valhalla, paying as much as $400.00 for a first edition copy on eBay. To him all twenty-five novels were his children and he loved them all for different reasons, but despite what was intrinsic learning for him, he must have realized that Bone was an excellent story done in fine literary style. Of course he had been too modest to admit anything of the kind.

I answered Mel, advising him to proceed apace and act according to what was in the best interests of the property, as George had always done and had instructed me to do as well. I then filled a few orders for books on line for amazon.com through the print on demand company, Lightning Source. It was becoming easier all the time to see that George's fans could receive books. My little piece of business complete, I got all dressed up and drove over to that beautiful castle I had seen from the gondola, The Banff Springs Hotel. Built during the time of construction of The TransCanadian Railways, the owner hoped this beautiful place would become a calling card for wealthy from around the world and he spared no expense. He was right. The little museum on the second floor was an homage to its past, housing everything from pictures of famous people to early menus and furniture. It was all quite grand with its marble floors, dark highly polished wood and vaulted ceilings, and I was grateful I'd dressed respectfully.

On the back of the brochure I had received upon entering the national park a few days earlier was an advertisement for Qivik, garments made from the finest wool in the world. The address on the bottom of the ad noted The Banff Springs Hotel, so I set out to find it. Plans were being made for my daughter, Leah's, wedding shower in the fall and I thought maybe a little vest would be a nice touch to wear with a simple blouse and skirt, as both my girls expected me to dress classically, which was their idea of a mother of the bride. My own view of clothes is that they are, first and last, costumes, but love for my girls will always help keep me socially appropriate. I walked into the lovely little shop on the first floor and headed right to the vests. There, on display, was just the one I'd seen! It certainly was soft and well made. The colors were delicately muted. It was on sale, too. I turned over the price tag; only $650.00.

"Can I help you?" Offered a well-manicured young woman.

"No, thanks, just looking." I smiled before leaving the shop. Sorry, girls, momma will have to find something else honorable to wear…

My hiking couple du jour was a young photographer and his wife, a school teacher who wrote children's books. If I thought I had been physically challenged the day before, today made that seem like a walk in the park. Over hill and dale the lively exertion was made bearable by the even livelier conversation. It was all about the arts and how much creative expression soothes our hearts. Jason had just finished his masters at the University of Edmonton. Subsequently they had hired him on as a professor. He was in Banff to meet with a colleague and they would be discussing techniques for photographing Banff in the old style of the first pictures ever taken of Banff by famous photographers. Jennifer taught third grade. Her latest book published was about the travails and hopes of her charges. Seemingly interested in George's works and my own we chatted on most amiably for the next hour. Jason's meeting was to be held 45 minutes after our walk and, since I knew they were tent camping, I'd offered them my RV to shower in. They had already made arrangements to clean up, but we agreed to leave a little time at the end of our jaunt to exchange e-mail addresses. I was looking forward to seeing his art work on line and satisfying my curiosity about Jennifer's children's book, if not purchasing one to hold onto in the off chance I might possibly have GRANDCHILDREN.

As we were coming up to the campgrounds at Tunnel Mountain I looked over to see exactly where I was in relation to The Nest. At that moment my toe caught a small stump and I fell forward down a minor decline. By the time Jason and Jennifer had leaned over to help me up I was back on two feet and brushing myself off. Since my body was already looking like that of a seven year old tom boy with all of the wacks and cracks I'd been getting by working with the RV, I reckoned a couple more scrapes and bruises wasn't going to matter. However, whether it was the arduous walk coupled with the heat or something else I couldn't explain, I was feeling very vulnerable and anxious to get 'home.'

I turned to Jason and Jennifer and said, "It was a pleasure to meet you both. Thank you very much for letting me join you on your walk today, but here's where I'll bid you both Adieu." I pointed toward The Nest. They seemed a little taken back but shook my hand and smiled graciously.

When they were about two hundred feet behind me I could hear them both laughing heartily. "What could they be laughing about?" I thought. Yes, I was that out of it. They probably wondered what they had said or done to have made me depart so abruptly without even exchanging e-mail addresses. I felt humiliated by my lack of social acuity as I hurried home to clean and wash my new open wounds.

Arlene and Wilf had invited me to hike with them in Telleman Trail but when I woke the next morning my lower back, which had been a little tender the past few days, seized up completely. The fall I had taken the previous day was probably the coup de gras. Interestingly, especially considering all of the worrying about my health I had been experiencing, I was not upset at all. I advised loved ones who were calling to check in on me that my back could have gone out whether I was in a house or in a motor home. Additionally, I loved it here and, although I was due to leave in two days, I knew there would be plenty of open spots at Tunnel Mountain if I needed to stay longer.

When I called Arlene and Wilf to beg off the sojourn they too had changed their minds about the hike since the night before it had rained heavily and the trail would be a mess. I took low dose pain pills leftover from when I had previously broken my wrist over the course of the next twenty-four hours and that helped relax the area tremendously. Enough so that in two days I was able to open up my front door and gingerly move about in the sunshine. In that time motor homes had come and gone and I now had new neighbors. The key would be to get my back to relax enough so that hooking up Maxine to the back of The Nest with the Blue Ox would not put additional strain on the area. I realized that I only needed to be able to travel nine hours over the next seven days to pick up Mimi in Seattle, which enabled me to just relax and enjoy Banff. And, oh, how I loved Banff! The rainy miserable days I had spent before I got here

seemed like a lifetime away.
August days in Banff were reminiscent of the late fall Indian Summers of New York I'd experienced in my childhood, deliciously cool mornings warmed up with a golden sun by late afternoons. Surely there are other places on this planet that can brag so delicious a combination, but it was like dining on the finest culinary meal; appreciating every sense to completely satisfy the human palate. It is no wonder that with all the experiences of hiking and meeting people and sleeping well and painting that I decided to throw my back out - just to stay a few days more! So magnanimous were Arlene and Wilf, so filled with promise the young photographer and children's writer; even the retired couple filled with fears were endeared to me as I felt compassion. Glorious wonder that is Banff, I am grateful for your healing!

*

"I LOOOOVE YOU!" George had bellowed across the field from the house to the beach where I was compounding a gash we'd made in the side of the catamaran.
"I'LL BE LOVING YOU AAAAALWAYS!" I shouted back in sing song glee.
For a man who never wanted to own a house or a car, or get married again, or have a pet,

George surely had experienced a complete turnabout in attitude! He had hocked me for two and a half years to marry him, more to keep in tune with the romance of his soul than any social considerations, although his concern for his literary estate was an occasional topic of conversation. When the opportunity to purchase our own home in upstate New York on The Hudson River presented itself George jumped at it even quicker than I, who *was* handy and willing. Living in so reclusive an area mandated we purchase a four wheel truck so that we wouldn't be held captive in the bad weather months. Daily he drove his pick up truck wearing a cheap black baseball cap with embroidered gold dragons he'd brought in China (just like the *other* guys on the tour bus had!) to get the newspaper and the mail, as there was no delivery service for either in our little bucolic town of New Baltimore. His faithful dog, Pig, sat sphinx-like in the seat next to him. I'd nicknamed him 'Bubba' and he loved it.

"Did you put the blow up mattress in the back of the truck?"

George was leaning against the railing of the deck, taking a break from the 'arduous' task of loading the car in his usual manner - by having a cigarette.

"Check." He answered in spit shine fashion.

"Did you put the heros and beer in the cooler?"
"Check." Then adding a little restlessly, "Are you almost done there?"
"What time is it?" I was hoping to buy another twenty minutes.
"Eight - and Pig's already nipped my ass once!"
That dog was so bossy! I realized that additional sanding and finishing touches on the catamaran would have to wait for another time. "I'm on my way up."
We had traded in our season tickets to The Metropolitan Opera House and New York City Ballet for the drive-in movies. On Tuesday nights we would take the truck to the outdoor theater on 9W, back it up in the front row, inflate the mattress so that we could lay on it in the flatbed and, together with his dog, his wife, a hero sandwich and a few beers George would joyously watch the latest alien or action movie. I would joyously watch him.

*

Every morning I resolved to take better care of myself. To eat healthier, drink more water and less booze, get plenty of exercise, take my vitamins, and most of all live in appreciation. All of these ambitions usually lasted until about four in the afternoon at which point, weary from the day's demands,

I would succumb to the child that was me, unwilling to consider the consequences I would unhappily suffer in disappointment the next day. Even saying 'unto all things there is a season' did not help me accept the fact that part of assuaging my sorrows, hurts, and humiliations of the day included a good stiff drink and food choices that were clearly not in my best interest, nor did it help me accept the guilt.

When the two couples traveling together in the beautiful RV across from me invited me over for dinner after they saw my predicament I heartily accepted. Once again, focaccia bread in hand, I anxiously knocked on their door at the appointed time and was warmly greeted. I was becoming a real social butterfly here!

Millie and Dave, traveling from California, had met up with their old friends LaDon and Ron and Michigan and offered them a rather spontaneous adventure. Gleeful in their newly discovered world of retirement, they had gratefully accepted and here, in Banff, they were before heading to Seattle where Dave would be giving a seminar. Obviously bright, erudite people, I enjoyed listening to their travel stories and they mine. If there was one recurring theme about motor home travel, I was discovering, it was that everyone had a story of near disaster. Wilf had taken off the steps leading up to the front door of his RV by forgetting to pull them up when leaving a site. Dave, not at all handy, couldn't even imagine my handling the Nest alone, as he depended upon Millie's help and had laughingly said, "Every morning before I get behind that wheel, I pray to God I don't kill myself or somebody else."

Not long into our glad-to-meetcha's the wonderful meal Millie had prepared was presented. Dave turned solemnly to me and said, "We say grace here, will you join us?"

"Of course," I responded respectfully.

His prayer was one of appreciation for the exchange of humanity between us all and the bounty we would be enjoying. Turns out Dave was a motivational speaker for ministers and Ron wrote educational materials on the topic. How interesting…

Not one time in the almost two hours I spent with these lovely people did they ask my religion or try to sell me theirs. It was a loving, joyous experience and later that evening I wondered if George would have been able to enjoy himself in their company.

That night, contemplating my time in Banff, I rested easy. Despite the fact that I'd be coughing I realized that I probably didn't have TB, and although my back still hurt it couldn't possibly be ovarian cancer. The chances of my getting a heart attack were probably very slim and, my latest, *exceptionally* dry nasal passages - well I hadn't figured that one out yet but I probably wouldn't die from it, either. Heck, I probably wouldn't even end up with the H1N1 flu…

Albertans say they have two seasons: winter and construction. Never was this more evident than taking The QEW from Banff through Lake Louise and into Yoho and Glacier National Parks. A ride that should have taken me three and a half hours elongated to four and a half hours, with only a brief stop at the Spiral Tunnels. Nonetheless, the drive had been spectacular. Wide but shallow milky-sage colored streams swirled around the bases of craggily, imposing mountains; some perpetually capped with snow. The early morning sunlight blessed this corner and then became more magnanimous until all was bathed in brightness. Further on roads, water and railway vied for elbow room, as all manner of transportation came through the narrow pass. The driving had become more precarious. I carefully chose moments to peek up and enjoy the scenery between dodging eighteen wheelers and careening sharp corners. One hard and fast rule developed quickly. The speed limit of 45 miles per hour meant 45 miles per hour. Period. Layers upon layers of mountains stretched out in front of me as I depressed the acceleration pedal to the floor in an attempt to squeeze out another five mph in the ascending. It was like trying to push an elephant up a slide. Even the fir trees looked like something Charlie Brown would bring home, struggling against the elements. Eventually glorious lakes spread out before me. To my surprise boats moored happily along the shores. It seemed as if nature had played a cruel trick on this beautiful landscape, as certainly the boating season could not be more than a few short months.

All of this splendor lifted my spirits, as having left Banff was a parting of sweet sorrow. Many new friends had been made and perhaps I'd peeled away another layer of the onion in trying to revamp my cynical view of humanity.

My back, still tender, was demanding attention so, satisfied with the day's drive, I stopped at Revelstoke in British Columbia, set my watch back another hour, and holed up in The Nest at a serviceable KOA. Having had such a fine experience at Shady Oaks with Ewan I was no longer the frightened pansy I'd been a mere three weeks ago. Here, on the other side of the mountains, was where all the heat and winds had been immobilized and an honest summer presented itself. The front of The Nest, with its expansive window, took on all the characteristics of a terrarium and I happily accommodated the feel by peeling off layers of clothing every couple of hours. I pressed on the next day and, seeing a tiny dot about forty-five minutes from the USA border that called itself 'Hope' I smiled, instincts prevailing, and headed toward it. *The Wild Irish Rose* was a lovely campground, managed by Roy and Bev. Bev, sporting a big red hat with a feather, insisted I help myself to the purple hydrangeas along the entrance that I'd admired, and later in the day brought me over a 'welcome' tomato from her garden. Roy and his minions were working hard to keep the place ship shape. All the sites were well shaded, pleasantly appointed and, as we nestled against the base of a vaulting mountain façade, life seemed to hold precious little worry. Since Bev knew I was traveling alone she asked me to join her on her morning walks, which consisted of navigating a strip of dirt along the town's main drag to get to the gas station/convenience store. Here she purchased her daily lottery ticket and whatever other little commodity she needed.

I was just happy for the company. Knowing I had close to a week before I had to be in Seattle, I set up my easel and became part of the meis en scene that was Hope, British Columbia.

Four days later I set Enumclaw, Washington, USA as my destination. I would be arriving two days before my reservation at Kanasta State Park and while I had enjoyed the wonderful peace of these last several weeks and meeting new people, I was looking forward to seeing Mimi again. An ebullient loving soul, she'd wanted to be part of my journey and I wanted it to be special for her. I looked forward to opening up the awning, setting out the canvas chairs and maybe even having a campfire.

It was disappointing to hear that the state parks in Seattle were so strapped for money that many of them were not manned at all during the week. While my phone call had been answered by a live person, the information I received was sketchy... *There probably would be something available. Just go in and drive around. If there are no 'reserved' stickers in front of a site I should just take it. There would be a box by the bathroom to put money in.*

Honestly, I'd have liked a little bit more to go on than that. Driving carefully through the winding narrow pathways I found myself in a camping section for tents and, despite my best effort to watch my ass, I ended up nipping a metal post in an attempt to retreat from the unfriendly area. The post was fine, The Nest was not. At least I hadn't broken a rear tail light. As soon as I found the motor home section and an unmarked spot, I settled down and pulled out the duct tape, which was quickly becoming my best friend.

Stocking up on food supplies turned out to be a joyous excursion, albeit thirty minutes away. The amenities one takes for granted on the West Coast are something we from the East can only dream of - aisles and aisles of great wines and fresh, inexpensive fruits and vegetables as far as the eye can see! Despite the full day's travels, disappointments at both leaving Canada and having so unceremonious a welcome in Seattle's camp grounds at Enumclaw, setting up camp and food shopping I still had enough energy to see that Maxine got a much needed car wash before bringing all the booty back to camp.

There was one more project I wanted to accomplish before settling down. I wanted to make the outside of The Nest an outdoor living space. I had never opened up my awning or set out the lovely carpet I'd purchased after admiring the brochures of

RVers who had made themselves comfortable in vacation style comfort. I knew Mimi would love a good roaring fire, which was something else I'd never experienced as I'd been too concerned about being out at night alone.

After a good hour's struggle between reading the brochure and some common sense guesstimates, I'd unfurled the awning, set up two canvas chairs on the carpet, and purchased wood from the campground store. I felt ready for company.

I've never been a woodsy person, but I can see the virtue of its relaxation appeal. Kind of like the difference between people who take drugs that are 'downers' as opposed to people who like 'uppers'. The River is for people, like George and me, who like uppers. We needed the power of The Hudson to stimulate us and give us strength. We relied on its ever changing tides and great undercurrent. The woods, I think, is for those who need downers. For the next two days I tried to sit tight. Staying here without a body of water was not as disturbing as I might have imagined, but it was hard for me to relax into the lack of action. The only movement that caught my eye for stimulation was an occasional bird or an ant. Chatter from other campsites was both welcome and annoying. The difficulty laid in not needing more but still my overriding fear of being harmed usurped any relaxation the place offered. A constant companion, a stellar jay pleased me because of its great joi de vive, but seemingly empty RV's spoke of possible madness, or drug deals as the case of one motor home which had a great deal of 'company' in and out, all day long. Or perhaps my perseveration was due to nothing more than an over active imagination. I think I'm overdue for the sane stability of my sister!

*

George's first marriage had been a disaster. Both George and Donna were teenagers and the relationship was fraught with volatility combined with alcohol. They had a son who was the light of George's life, but in the end mother and son went out west and George saw the boy three times in his entire adult life. George faired no better in his second attempt at marriage to Ori and, despondent with his failures, retreated into his hermitage on The Hudson. Over the fifteen years he spent there his obsessive compulsive disorders increased, having no mechanism to keep them minimized he got worse. He locked the front door twenty times or more each night, checked the faucets for leaks with little hand motions, touched pictures, books, and wall cornices he passed with ritualistic fervor, ate specific meals at specific times on specific days of the week, made copious lists of television programs he would tape, chess games he played, and submissions of his works for possible publication. Thank goodness he could control the worlds he created while writing! He had worked with severely disturbed teenagers at Rockland Psychiatric Center when money from writing wasn't enough to pay the bills and would tell the teens that the difference between them and him was that he knew how to take care of business in order to live in the outside world. It was his goal to teach them how to be able to do that.

*

Chapter Seven

Mimi is here! I picked her up at SeaTac Airport, tickled pink to realize that it was only a half hour's drive from the state park. Her plane had landed early and, as always, she was easy to spot. Even curbside in the dark Mimi exuded an energy I couldn't miss. She had spotted the car and was waving eagerly.

Pulling into the pick-up area, I rolled down the window of the passenger side. "Boy, are you a sight for sore eyes!" The heartfelt pronouncement of my exclamation surprised even me.

Despite eight hours of travel after a long hard day's work, Mimi's laugh was a delicious blend of chimes and love. I hopped out of the car and we met each other for an embrace by the trunk.

She enveloped me in a strong hug before pulling back to take a hard look. "You look great, my darlin'." Her wide, dark eyes of chocolate reflected back to me the deep soul that she was.

"Thanks, Pussycat. You, too!" I fairly beamed.

Mimi was the tallest girl in our family, topping out at 5'7", and with her long, ever shining dark straight hair, was, for my

money, the most gorgeous of us all. This fact had caused me great jealousy when I was a child and I considered myself lucky that she loved me, as I had not always been kind. "You've lost weight since I saw you last!" I noticed encouragingly.
"Workin on it, Girl." She answered as she hoisted her luggage up and over the bumper and into the trunk.
The airport was, thankfully, easy to exit and before long we were headed towards Kanasta State Park, our home for the next two days.
"Look!" Mimi excitedly pointed up to the sky. There, straight ahead, was a full and brilliant moon. "George is with us, tonight!" She exclaimed with awe in her sing-song voice.
The bittersweet that is memory washed over me, making it difficult for the moment to concentrate on driving.
About two months after George had died I went through a torturous period, knowing I had to leave the home that was ours but miserable about the decision. I was terrified that I would be leaving George behind, as The Hudson River was his great source of power and I imagined it to be my forever reminder of him. One night at about three in the morning I was woken by a light so bright it was as if someone driving down the

hill to our house had the high beams of their car lights on and was shining them into the bedroom through the two inch opening of the drapes. Three-quarters asleep I tried to focus on the highly unlikely abnormality only to realize that the brilliance was not coming from the narrow roadway, but from atop the cliff and was sitting perfectly on the western horizon. It was a full moon, huger than any I had ever seen before or since and, in the softest, calmest voice imaginable, George had said to me, "I am here. I will always be with you wherever you go. Rest easy and do not worry." I had fallen back asleep immediately.

"Yes, yes, he is," I said softly, before my throat closed.

We both said our silent 'hellos' to George The Moon and then Mimi patted my arm. Determinedly and with great effort I did not cry.

Instead, I addressed Mimi's hunger issue. "What kind of pasta do you want?" When we spoke two days earlier about what she wanted me to pick up for her from the supermarket she had told me to just have the pasta ready. I figured she would arrive starving and be looking for a hearty meal, despite the late hour.

"Pasta?" She answered quizzically.

"Yeah, didn't you tell me on the phone to

have the pasta ready?"
Mimi roared for about ten seconds before finding her voice. "The *vodka*, Girl, I said just have the *vodka* ready!"
Oh. Right. Of course. I joined in her laughter.
I was sorry it was so dark out, for surely Mimi would be impressed with how beautiful the park was. I drove confidently, turning right and left through the grounds I was now familiar with.
"Good God! We're in the middle of nowhere!" Mimi's voice, usually strong, sounded a little shaky. I imagined she was feeling like a stranger in a strange land, exacerbated by a long hard day of travel.
"It's gorgeous, Mim, you're going to love it in the sunshine. Tomorrow we can go into Seattle or if you prefer, just stay in the park and do some hiking along the river. There's class four rapids not far from here." Mimi is an outside kind of gal and my money was on her choosing the rustic rather than city experience. I knew that feeling of disjointed alienation she was experiencing and so I did my best to allay her fears by outlining the intended route I'd planned for us and by hyping up our adventure. "Saturday morning we'll head south into Oregon. We have a reservation in the Willamet Valley area." One of the objects of our time

together was to visit the wineries, which Mimi had never done and I believed would be a wonderful education for us both.
"Sounds great." Mimi replied, making an honest attempt at her usual enthusiasm.
"Then we'll take the coastal route south, 101, and when we get to California, we'll go into the redwood forests. Our reservation is at The Jedediah State Park."
"Sweet!" She was sounding better.
"We have two days to meander south before our reservation in Calistoga, where we'll hit the mud baths and do the Napa Valley winery tours."
I lost a little ground there, as she mused aloud. "Mud baths? O.k. whatever. I trust you."
I laughed. "You're going to love it."
We were interrupted by a full view of The Nest, compliments of Maxine's headlights. "We're here!" I stated the obvious, pulling in behind the RV. We made quick work of unloading the car and climbed aboard Mimi's home away from home for the next ten days.

Mimi held out two, small and identical rubberized orange items. I was in the middle of showing her where the sheets and blankets were for the pull out couch on which she would be sleeping when they appeared in her outstretched hand. I had no idea what they were or why she was offering them to me.

My lost look made her giggle. She looked absolutely shy and a little unsure of herself, neither of which would be considered a Mimi trait. She spoke, haltingly, as if rehearsed. "I made up my mind. I want to sleep with you."

'Sweetie Pie!" I responded, deeply touched. I quickly searched for a reason why this wouldn't work for me but couldn't come up with a single one. Certainly there would be plenty of room for both of us to sleep in the queen sized bed. The additional bonus, of course, would be the fact that we would be able to talk into the night. "O.k., let's do it!" I'd said enthusiastically.

The two orange thingies were ear plugs.

The following morning Mimi did the most unexpected, amazing thing. She opened up the window shades. Sun streamed into my little home for the first time since I'd left New York. My initial reaction was one of vulnerability, to tell her to shut them; but I realized quickly that what she had done was exactly the right thing to do. I now had a travel mate and the fears associated with soloing the journey could be set aside. More importantly, the metaphor was not lost on me. Light in my life - what a concept!

*

George's writing was slowing down. It was actually a dream of his *not* to have to write in order to feel emotionally stable, so I was glad for him. He used to say "Happy people don't write." Gauging from other writers I had met on the few occasions when we had been invited to France by Francois Gueriff, George's French publisher and a great bear of a man whom we both adored, I would readily attest to George's observation. It also appeared to me that alcoholism was a common thread amongst the literatie. Now, I'm not talking about formulaic, successful writers. I'm talking about struggling, mid-list authors who are well respected for literary styles, but are not invested in by large publishing companies who are looking for broad-based audiences so that they can get the biggest bang for their advertising buck. If you hadn't written a break out book by your third attempt you were relegated into this remainder bin. George was the in good company of strong writers, but he was always hopeful that someday one of his novels would make it to 'the big screen'.

He woke at five a.m. every morning, put up a pot of coffee and had a cigarette outside on the deck. There, leaning heavily against the railing with both elbows supporting his cigarette and chin, he would watch the sun's earliest rays sweep magenta across the diurnal sky and reflect off the glass-like waters of the morning Hudson. While George bathed in appreciation for the wonder that was Life, Pig inspected his land for possible night intruders, abluted and peed instinctively. Both satisfied with their day's beginnings, George would come into the house and sit in his 'thinking' chair with his 'thinking' baseball cap on, determined to come up with a great new idea. Pig lay beside him, hoping to help in any way he could. Alas, the fireflies were laying dormant. There were no sparks of imagination or inspiration. Day after day George would sit in his great chair until he fell back asleep, pad on his lap and his right hand atop Pig's head, stilled in mid-pet. Unfortunately, George was now a happy man and true to his own observation, he did not write.

*

The next two days were a delicious blur of laughter and gravitas as Mimi and I shared stories about work, family, and the community in which we both were raised; the community in which Mimi still resided. We bemoaned relationships gone by the wayside and recounted joyous times. We hiked, ate well at times, ate poorly at others,

and slept side by each. By the time we finally left Enumclaw, Washington, we were ready for the long drive that lay ahead.
Traveling south to Eugene, Oregon was unimpressive and uneventful, except for the tremendous amount of traffic around an outlet mall that added an additional hour to our trip. We pulled into the campground at 4:30 and hustled, taking quick showers and changing before heading out to the wineries on our itinerary which we knew would be closed by 6:30. We made it to two. The first experience, by far the best, was King's Estate; Spanish architecture, spectacular views of the vineyards, and delicious tastings were a fabulous way for Mimi to be welcomed into the world of west coast wineries. Ira, the somalier who poured the wines and spoke of their varying attributes, couldn't help but notice our New York accents.
"Let me guess. Thirty miles north of Manhattan, say, Rockland County?"
That was astounding. Had we filled out any paperwork when we entered that may have left a trail for a psychic? Nope.
"Monsey!" Mimi answered excitedly.
"Me, too!" He said in mock enthusiasm.
"Grandview Avenue," Mimi pushed the geographical envelope.
"Forshay Road," he countered.

"That's less than a mile away!" Mimi, on her first trip to the west coast, appeared to be meeting a neighbor.
"Left fifteen years ago and haven't been back since."
Small world.
The second winery was wedged in between the railroad tracks and the local prison. It was more of a wine bar but we were assured by the bartender that the grapes, while grown some fifteen miles east, were actually processed there. We were not impressed with the wine but asked for a recommendation of a good place for dinner. That proved more fruitful and twenty minutes later we were in The Eugene Station House which had been remodeled into a lovely restaurant where we had a quick bite before heading back to The Nest.

White knuckle driving is the only way to describe our coastal trip south through Oregon and into The Californian Redwood Forests. Eighteen wheelers whizzed passed us on the narrow, windy road to Jedediah Smith Redwood State Park. Our only stop for the day had been for local customs at the Californian border. Inspectors, upon seeing my New York license plates, insisted on checking our undercarriage for moth nests, vigilant against possible devastation the moths could wreak in the forests. We assured them, straight faced, that we would indeed contact them if we saw any subsequent sign of the pesty critters.

Once again The Park was no match for The Nest. I realize that both state and federal parks were laid out long before the 32 foot RV showed up on the circuit, but how about at least taking out a stump or two. The pull-through site they had assured me over the phone could accommodate us was bursting at the seams like a fat lady in small corset, barely able to contain The Nest. Mimi insisted on learning how to remove the tow bar, so we made quick work of that project in order to park Maxine elsewhere. Despite how dark it was under the canopy of redwood branches, we still had enough daylight to hike through the park and into The Enchanted Forest. I was glad Mimi brought her camera. We felt like miniature dolls against the massive trunks, trying to get as much of a tree in the picture as possible in order to accurately portray the size. Having had our fill of hiking and having worked up a good appetite, we headed back to our campsite where Mimi informed me that she would make a fire and cook the Tbone we had on tap. It was tough going but she persevered and within the hour, in the dark of an earthy night, we enjoyed a perfectly done steak by the light of the twitching embers. As I lay beside Mimi that night, her earplugs in and eye mask on, I began to talk. I started benignly enough but as my concept of the time passing warped I spoke more freely about those personal things between a man and a woman one may never share with another during their life. Things that usually follow us into our graves. A man might consider this 'kiss and telling' but to a woman who has lost her husband the ache to share and be consoled by another woman she trusts with her heart is a catharsis that is difficult to explain to a man without a feminine sensibility. I don't even think I stopped talking after I distinctly heard Mimi snore.

I was a grouch. I admit it. It had been another white-knuckle driving day. Construction and traffic made the going even harder and, while Mimi and I had a great time 'oohing' and 'aahing' every time we rounded a bend in appreciation of the scenic views before us, after seven hours of driving I was shot. Additionally, Greta Garmin could not have imagined The Nest would have been so unresponsive to her demands to keep up with the speed limits. As a result, we were not going to make it all the way to Callistoga this day. Mimi, fully vested after taking her final vows as Navigator, scanned the map for the closest town and looked for a campground in the Woodalls Camping book. Despite a notation that the respite was only four miles off Route 12, I could not believe how long it took us to get there. Windy, narrow roads and steep inclines, even the owners knew they were asking a lot of us campers as we read a huge, hand printed sign on the side of the road that read, "You're Almost There!" And, to add insult to injury, it was $55.00 a night! The manager began to tell me that the pull through sites were more when I turned to Mimi and said, "Let's continue south. I can do another hour or so."

The short, blonde woman behind the counter did not wait to read the look of horror on Mimi's face, immediately capitulating in the face of my bluff. "Its late enough in the day to know that the pull-through will be unused. You can have it for the same price."

Satisfied that a bargain had been struck, I paid the extortionist while Mimi, ever ebullient, chatted on amiably about how well kept the grounds were and what a phenomenal view of vineyards the campers must enjoy. I suppose I should have been more ashamed of myself but I couldn't muster up the guilt, muttering to Mimi on the way to our site that I wasn't the first or the last miserable traveler to have pulled in here. Enjoying a glass of wine in the hot tub an hour later helped to assuage my bad temper.

After a good night's sleep Mimi and I woke fresh and ready to hit the road. I waved madly to the manager on the way out with a big fat smile on my face and giving her the 'thumbs up' for the experience. A little overcompensation of appreciation.

An hour and a half later we arrived at the Calistoga RV Campground next to the Fairgrounds, which resembled an old drive in movie theater without the screen. It was, however, a mere grape's throw away from the three wineries we had decided to visit. Our first order of business, however, was the famous Dr. Watkin's Mud Bath House.

Our side-by-each appointment for the medicinal bath and massages was set for two p.m. Anyone who has never been to the mud baths is surely missing out on one of life's more uncomfortable pleasures. Uncomfortable because the bath is a hot mushy mess of wine renderings, seeds, and twigs in a floamish bog set into a sarcophagus-like cement rectangle. Completely undressed, a condition I noticed with some surprise Mimi was distinctly unhappy about, we wriggled ourselves as far down into the mash as we could while the matron covered us with additional 'mud'. After placing cucumbers on our eyes and 'salad dressing' on our faces we were instructed to smile so that our photograph could be taken. I was not sure if Mimi would make that little memento the cover page of her vacation album, but we complied. I could hear the timer being set and the minutes ticked away slowly as the poisons were unceremoniously sucked from our beings. It took longer to try and wash the grit out of our every orifice, but in case Dr. Watkin's crew ran into slackards without the mandated hygiene, we were next dropped like dumplings into a bubbling caldron of lilac water. Copious amounts of ice water with lemon slices for us to drink kept presenting themselves wherever our right hand set down, as replenishing the body's water supply was an essential part of the cleansing process.

Being one of eight children, I'd lost all sense of modesty fifty years ago and had assumed my sister would have felt the same, but the ten minute sauna was another source of humiliation for the naked Mimi, the poor chickie! I just closed my eyes pretending to be completely absorbed in the experience that was scorching heat. The massage afterwards, while deliberate and intense, was like a walk in the park compared to the previous torture and I do believe that in the end Mimi paid gratuities to her torturers with less of a whimper than I might have expected, under the circumstances.

One might imagine that after undergoing such rigor that Mimi and I would have calmly returned to The Nest and continued the regimen of healthful living and purity. One would be wrong. As soon as the last breath of Dr. Watkins Mud Bath was exhaled, we zipped as quick as two clean bunnies to Sterling, a winery five minutes from Dr. W's that my daughter, Rachael, had touted. We hoped to ride the gondola to the top of the mountain where the processing plant was situated and have a wine tasting before they closed the doors. The wine gods were with us - we just made it. A little education, a little wine, a lot of great scenery and, as always, the great company of my Mimi, the day was delicious and healing. We capped off the day with dinner at one of the flagship restaurants, The Calistoga Inn, by sharing an horsdeurve and a pasta dish. After that experience we decided to share our wines in the future, too. After all, we were beginning to learn about why certain wines make for great pairings with certain foods and we wanted to experience the full Monte!

*

Squirrel monkeys can be pretty darn horny. George and I laughed as the little guy lay belly up on the picnic table beside us. Clearly he was making eyes at me and as I began to tickle the inside of his extended arm he got a little erection. Well, maybe not little for him, this I don't know, but George began to howl. My new pint-sized boyfriend did not care for George's attitude and, having now lost his 'intentions' towards me, he began to focus on revenge. He scampered upon George, scaling him like a small bush, landing fully atop his head and grabbing what little hair George had left in each hand. To that point we had been quite amused, but when the little guy 'switched sides' and began humping George's head I was the only one howling. I'd never seen George move so fast, as he bolted from the table swinging his arms wildly. Overpowered, the little monkey gave up on us and scampered away down the elevated boardwalk. Another five seconds and George would have been wearing hair gel he hadn't applied himself! Later in the day, as we lazily played a half-hearted game of chess, a mischievous relative of our earlier playmate swiped my rook, running off quicker than you could say Guests At The Ariua Jungle Are Slow

Witted.
We had loved The Amazon, reveling in the potent energy that is The Rive Negre. We went hunting for Caymen by flashlight at night in the smaller waterways, piranha fishing in the early morning hours, and hiked the primordial forest receiving lectures on the bounty that is our great earth's treasures. At night we slept in hammocks that had been set up in our 'cage', for in the jungle we were the zoo pets and were eerily aware of all the pairs of eyes in the dark observing us with a predator's interest; the joys and mysteries of our planet never ceasing to amaze us!

*

Even wineries can be pretty kitschy when it comes to entertaining the hoards of visitors they have to entertain each year. That is not to say the experiences weren't pleasant, it is just that many of the tours lacked a certain authenticity. In many ways it was like going to the Animal Kingdom in Disney World as opposed to a safari in South Africa. It's still a good time, just contrived.
Mimi and I spent the next two days tooling around Napa, tasting and learning, and even treating ourselves to a wonderful little luncheon at The Culinary Institute. We did the mandatory shopping in each of the little boutiques, as she looked about feverishly

hoping to find something honorable to bring back to loved ones. It was easier for me to 'just say no' to shopping, unimpressed with the sport and defaulting on my rather cheap attitudes to start with. Mimi, however, whimpered about what might possibly fit in her luggage until I acquiesced, once again, to forgo my 'travel light travel far' mentality and assured her that I would stock her wares under the kitchen bench. Then all bets were off.

Since Mimi was one of those rare, extraordinarily fortunate women who'd married to a phenomenal cook, she had finally discovered an expertise she could bring to the table - literally and figuratively! She bought wines at almost every winery, studying with a passion akin to the great perfumers of Europe. It was joyous to watch her revel in each swirl of the wine glass' base, each deep intense smell - the look on her face reflective and hopeful. Could she smell all of the scents each somalier bragged? Would she be able to savor the lingering taste? From Pinot Grigios to Cab Francs and all variations in between, we sipped and spit, hoping to fit one more winery in before closing time each day.

Our last stop of our last evening was at Peju, chosen again on a recommendation. We were immediately struck by the sculptures and creative gardens welcoming us. A sweet, warm breeze coupled with a still-warm sun, low on the horizon, swept the aroma of roses through us. By the time we reached the entrance doors our rushed attitude had abated. We were deliciously relaxed. Approximately a dozen of us late day tourists were ushered into an art gallery like bar, resplendent with vaulted ceiling and meticulously placed lighting. Our somalier, Henry, was brilliant, playing us all like little baby instruments in his symphony of Ode To Joyous Customers. We laughed easily at his jokes and tried earnestly to witness the ambiguous terms he used to describe their wines. I began to realize that, while extremely informative, Henry was actually selling us sensuality in a bottle. During our last tasting of the set spirits were high and, having been asked to take pictures of other couples using the tapestry artwork as background, I reveled in the task, joking lightheartedly with each grouping and making faux-serious work of the otherwise mundane requests.

A gentleman I had not observed as part of our group approached me quietly. He was a slight, well dressed man; handsome and dark with a comfortable smile and deep, warm brown eyes. I smiled back.

His accent was ever slight. "They say when you fall in love with a wine you cannot help but fall in love with the man who introduces you to that wine, as well."

Oh, my goodness, now *that's* a line to take home to momma! I like to think I was quick in my response. "Yes, I can feel that happening. That's why I'm on my guard with Henry, here," I said nodding my head in the somalier's direction, and then adding, "he's quite the charmer, you know!"

I do believe there was a bit more to the exchange with this unassuming man, but I do not recall it, whether due to wine or the impact of the statement. I do, however, seem to recall receiving a long hard look before he left my side and the room, but I cannot be certain.

Mimi was giving me the 'wallawalla' eyes, raising her eyebrows up and down. I was just looking for someplace else to put my eyes. They rested on Henry. He was giving me a great grin.

"Do you know who that was?" He asked sporting a great Cheshire cat grin.

"No," I answered warily. Should I know the stranger?

"That was Mr. Peju." Henry seemed quite tickled to be the bearer of a latent introduction.

"Sweet!" I responded all agog.

Mimi and I couldn't wait to get outside and text Rachael the big news. "Mr. Peju was hitting on me!" I exclaimed in the text message. The fact that Rachael did not respond was meaningless to me for two reasons. First of all, she's constantly rolling her eyes at my over exaggeration of my sexual prowess and self-importance. Secondly, Mimi and I were feeling rather sexy and self-important so we really didn't care. We went to a fabulous restaurant that Henry had recommended and, as a grand, golden sun set lazily on the horizon of the vineyard where we dined, we shared both meals and wines, like the pros we were.

The traffic from Napa to San Francisco was pretty light so we made it to Candlestick RV Park in what my son in law considered record timing; actually he called me a liar. It was, relatively speaking, expensive, but we were happy to be in the heart of San Fran and, I guess, that is what we were paying for. The park consisted mainly of men in construction who used the campground as a base for their work week and went home to their families on the weekend. There were a few transient campers like us, but mostly the men paid by the month or the season. It was an interesting three days and had we not been sightseeing and spending our time with

Rachael and Andrew I'm sure the fellows would have proved to be entertaining.

Mimi and I drove around Sausalito, crossing the Golden Gate Bridge to get there just as the fog rolled in. It is every bit the spectacle that has already been written about and remarked upon. She texted a picture of herself with the massive edifice behind her to her beloved husband, Paul, who was by the week's end beginning to sound like quite the whiner. He missed her terribly. She also texted the pic to her boss. Both responded jealously within five minutes.

Not uncruelly, she had snickered when responding back to Paul. It is always easier to be the one away on vacation than the one left at home!

Later that day we visited Rachael and Andrew in their brand new apartment on Mission Rock Road, two blocks away from the new stadium. They were happy to show us every nook and cranny, as it was the first time in their four years together that they needed to buy their own furnishings and they were quite proud of their joint venture. The four of us had dinner at one of the finest tourist traps on the wharf, heading out to a coffee bar afterwards. The only pall in an otherwise delicious day, was when we walked into the coffee bar the guitar duet was playing Chasing Cars, a song George and I identified with deeply. It was dark in there and I'm pretty sure no one saw my little dribbly tears, or if they did they were kind enough to let me have them without remark.

Chapter Eight

I really wasn't sure what I was going to do next. I had gotten as far as "…and Mimi will join me in Seattle and we will drive down to San Francisco." Now I was here. Now Mimi was leaving.

Rachael had asked me to stay with her the following week while she had a small operation performed, since Andrew would be out of town. I had said yes, but certain I wouldn't stay in Candlestick. I looked on a map for someplace on the ocean and decided I liked the name of Half Moon Bay, forty-five minutes southwest. Three hours after final hugs and kisses with Mimi at the airport I had cleaned out The Nest and began the relocation.

It had been a while since I'd had one of those huge breakdown cries about how painful life was without George and I imagined that since the great diversion of love and fun that was Mimi had left I was back to facing my loss. I thought about the few times I had been with other people and how it helped me forget about myself. This was a good thing and a bad thing. Certainly there was a tremendous desire, maybe even a self-protecting genetic need, to move past pain and look to the future, but still I wanted to feel my loss without using others to try and escape it. What did I expect? That the pain could leave so abruptly without a return engagement? The tears did not ebb until I had entered the outskirts of the little town. Even so, I didn't pay much attention to the magnificient meisen scene as I entered Pelican Point.

Content to be on the water, by my second day I was feeling rested and satisfied to be alone. I drove Maxine into Half Moon Bay, where wondrous orchid farms and herb gardens and bodegas with unusual sights and smells welcomed me. Once there I felt the healing of the plant life that surrounded me and my spirits lifted. Maxine reaped the rewards of my good mood by receiving a car wash.

Rachael and Andrew came for dinner and, now feeling restored, I asked them if there was any place they would like to go in the RV for the weekend before Andrew went to Dallas on business. An avid astronomer and photographer, he immediately chose Lake Sonoma. It was of high elevation, promising a spectacular vantage point. I eagerly began to contemplate my next little adventure and, as soon as they left, called the national park to make a reservation. They advised me that a reservation would not be necessary and that my stay there would have to be primative. That meant there would be no hookups, no facilities whatsoever. Even the bathrooms had been closed. One hundred degrees and you were on your own - no wonder you didn't need a reservation! The sting of this arrangement was offset by the ten dollar a day fee.

I knew I could keep the refrigerator running as well as cook with the propane, but my concern was for the electrical outlets and air conditioning, which would require use of the generator. Not having utilized the generator since purchasing The Nest I figured I should make sure it was in working order. The following morning I attempted to start it. To my consternation I had no success. I called Jen, back at Albany RV, and once, again, she did not let me down. There was a generator dealer about twenty-minutes from where Rachael worked, in Oakland. Preparations were made for me to go there in two days time.

My last morning at Pelican Point I woke to the sound of soughing waves. Their beckoning urged me to leave The Nest and return to the beach. The breezes wafted intermittently warm and cool so deliberately separate that if you could see them the atmosphere would look striated. Sitting on the water's edge, I wrote Robin & George with my finger inside a heart I'd etched in the wet sand. The irony that tide and time would erase it all was not lost on me. Adding to this feeling of morose, a young couple holding hands walked barefoot along the beach together, completely oblivious to their inevitable, doomed fate.

Unsure of how much time I had spent in this state of mind I decided it was time to leave the beach. I took one last, long look at The Pacific Ocean, wondering when, if ever, I would see it again.

*

Every afternoon at three o'clock George went to the local ice cream stand. He had a crush on the girl who worked there in the summertime.

"Today's special is chocolate swirl with walnuts and colored jimmies," she would announce after opening the window. A regular customer, she knew anything chocolate was his favorite.

George was initially shy and dropped his eyes at the sight of her every time. "That sounds good." He ventured a little further, "Do you have any whipped cream?"

"Of course!" She waited a minute for the joy to register before adding, "How would you like a fudge or butterscotch topping on that as well?"

Pleased as punch to be so well taken care of

George would smile broadly. "Fudge!"
"Alright, now. Would you like that in a cone or in a cup?"
"A cone, and a cherry on top!" George wanted it all and he welcomed it all with great enthusiasm.
After having made his final decision, George would yawn, for he had just woken from a two hour nap, which was indeed tiring. This was why he needed his snack. It was sustenance to carry forth.
"How have you been?" The ice cream girl would ask him in a flirtatious manner. Obviously she was as smitten with George as he with her.
"I'm doing woooonderful," George's charming affectation was enhanced with a smirk that could be mistaken for nothing if not sexy. He would wiggle his ears for her, happy to show off a talent.
By the time he had licked the end of his dripping ice cream cone his charm and humor had pleased them both.
As always, they enjoyed each other's company but never having ventured over the line of doting customer and sweet ice cream girl, the relationship remained achingly unexplored but enduring.
I often wondered if he would someday invite me out to a movie, but it didn't happen. Oh, how my heart pined for the handsome

customer who came to the ice cream shop where I worked every afternoon at three p.m.!

*

Winding road - up, up, up. Winding road - down, down, down. Cyclists and hikers, up and down. Attention must be paid going to Anthony Chabot! And it is worth every hair raising turn.

Satisfied with a new fuel pump for the generator and the quickness with which the dealership expedited the matter, my trek to the campground was, by necessity fiercely focused but relaxed. Greta Garmin was way out of her league, adding minutes to the estimated time of arrival faster than an airport during a snow storm. I let her off the hook without a moment's chastise, as the vista from atop the mountain were spectacular and the entrance to the park bucolic.

The first thing that struck me about the high, heavily wooded park was its smell. You cannot miss the deliciousness that hangs, permeating the atmosphere for miles. Having set up my hookups I sat at the proffered picnic table and tried to identify the familiar smell to no avail. In the end it was another camper who helped me out.

A raven haired woman walked her

Pomeranian past my site at just the right moment for me to sing out the question, "What *is* that delicious smell?"

"Eucalyptus!" She sang back.

Now I'm used to eucalyptus coming in the form of little dry branches that sit nicely in a vase and perfume your bedroom, so I began to scan the ground looking for the delicate, powdery leaves.

"The *trees* are eucalyptus," she'd added, noticing my confusion.

She reigned in the frisky little Pomeranian. "They aren't indigenous to California, though. They were brought here from Australia."

"Well, they sure are happy here now!" I noticed with amazement how prolific they had become, the entire area thick with the peeling, wooded trunks.

With a smile and a wave, the woman permitted the little Napoleon dog to have its way and the two continued their walk-about.

I liked it here. The sites were set comfortably apart from each other, affording the type of privacy I'd missed at Half Moon Bay. And while I'd been sad to leave the beach and little town, there was a peace about this place that spoke to me. It was at that moment that I had a baby epiphany. I thought, "*Every* place has its own happy little personality, the trick was being able to appreciate it." And a very new concept; "*Every* place is my home," began to form. As if solidifying this idea further, when I woke the next morning, for the first time since my journey began, I did not ask in the usual disoriented state, "Where am I?"

I made reservations to return to Anthony Chabot the following week before leaving for Lake Sonoma early Friday morning. Rachael and Andrew would be joining me later that night, once they finished their work week and braved through the northbound traffic. I didn't expect them before seven p.m.

Many from the San Francisco area took Fridays off from work to beat out the traffic into Napa and Sonoma Valley and I hustled along with them. There were lots of fancy cars on the road. I mused about fancy things; like a fast little navy-grey convertible with red bucket seats. Who would buy me such a toy? If Mr. Peju insisted on showering me with gifts that I really didn't need then that would have to be one of them. No, I mused further. Mr. Peju, in the hopes that I would marry him, would need to give me greater gifts. What did I want from the man who adored me beyond all measure? The man who simply could not buy me enough, do enough for me, professing his love grander than that ever before experienced? I thought a nice gesture would be for him to name his two greatest wines, from his signature collection of course, after my daughters. That seemed very generous of him. I sighed contentedly as I realized that I would probably need to buy fancy clothes now for all of the entertaining we would be doing, and I would have to hire a decorator to revitalize the rooms his unattended home must surely be suffering from. After all, he was a man dedicated to producing the finest wine, never looking up from his tastings... Now Mr. Peju would dedicate his life to taking good care of me...

*

I had never so much as drawn a stick figure in my entire life, but I believed George when he said I was a creative soul and just needed to find my medium of expression. Having spent so many years as a high achiever it was difficult for me to even take on a hobby without feeling that I had to excel at it, but we used words like 'warm and safe and dry and secure' to describe our little world. Judgment and failure were words that had been losing their impact for the past several years, enough so that I could take a chance. He brought me a phenomenal camera with all the fancy attachments so that I might capture the essence of our travels, and I enjoyed photography, but in the end it was oil painting that I embraced. Feeling strongly motivated, I began to take classes not far from the house and thoroughly immersed myself in the art of trying to achieve the look of a three dimensional still life on a two dimensional canvas. I realized to my great surprise that true creativity, was about the joy of expression and that while the honing of talent is immensely satisfying, the act of painting was the goal in itself. George, for all his encouragement, reveled in my every brush stroke. If I asked for his critique he was honest and loving, taking care not to blow out the tiny flame that was my self-protecting heart and, to that end, I must say every day I felt closer and closer to the six year old little girl that was Me. Shy and tentative I learned to take chances in self-exploration, sometimes it was a messy proposition but it was always rewarding. We were never disheartened by the four o'clock setting sun of a January or February day; fifteen feet apart from each other George wrote and I painted, usually to the soothing music of Puccini or Verdi.

"I'm lonely and need attention!" George would say loudly enough for me to hear. I would stop whatever I was doing and eagerly go to him.

"It's been a long time between kissells!" I would announce. George would stop whatever he was doing and come to me, open armed and smiling.

And, as always, we chorused each other with, "I'll be loving you aaaalllways!"

The only reason we wished we were perfect was so that *then* we would never hurt each other.

It wasn't until Leah stayed with us for six weeks while interning at Albany Medical Center that I came to understand the full import of the peace our lives had created. Her mother's daughter, my Leah lived the tension-filled high-achieving life I'd previously thought was so important, but within a few short days of living in our world she succumbed to the great gentleness. George and I watched the tension leave her like an ugly virus. We watched her heal and, as the great processor of new information that she was, we watched her learn how to heal her heart with self-compassion; as we had learned how to heal ourselves. It seemed obvious to us that this newfound understanding, not all of the financial and social accomplishments she would certainly experience, would be her greatest strength.

That, to us, was what taking care of each other was all about.

*

Lake Sonoma was as hot as blazes! The little brown office where the hostess resided in at Liberty Glen Campground had air conditioning, though. I know this because when she opened the window a great, but short-lived, rush of cold air whisked by me. I mention this because it seemed like cheating. If there are no facilities for us then there should be no facilities for them, I say. Looking a little sheepish, or maybe it was just my imagination, Ms. Kiosk promised me the only site in the camp that had a tree to offer some respite from the sun. I thanked her profusely. There was no point in grousing. With only the two of us in the entire park twenty miles from civilization we might need each other during a buzzard attack.

There were no pull throughs at the park so I had to disconnect Maxine on the only straight away of pavement there was, a quarter of a mile away from my assigned site. My kingdom for some shade and a modicum of air movement. Oh, Glory Be, Andrew and Rachael owe me big time! On the bright side, transporting myself about had now become easier. I decided to do a little food shopping in 'town' and find out where exactly one swam at Lake Sonoma; it certainly wasn't within walking distance of

the campground.
The shopping center surprised me, with its wide aisles and glorious food choices. I happily planned the weekend meals around such bounty, feeling well-stocked and ready for the discerning palates of my guests. The late afternoon swim was a more trying matter.
First of all, there were only three parking spaces allocated for cars - all the rest were earmarked for boat trailers with their towing vehicles. The little man at the entrance had been very clear that I could count on getting a rather pricey ticket for illegal parking, as the police came around constantly. All three spots were taken (surprise, surprise) and I would have to park a quarter mile away. Secondly, accessing the water's edge involved navigating a steep, treacherous descent, half of which was well over a hundred wood railroad tie 'steps' unevenly placed with a metal railing waist high that one could hold onto for stability. After that you were on your own over a rocky topography, not as steep but certainly far enough away to cause pause. Although I felt rather confident in getting to the water I was not as sure I had the tremendous exertion of energy that would be necessary to get back up to the parking lot. In the end the overwhelming desire to cool off

overpowered my apprehensions. My skin was so hot by the time I walked into the gravelly bottomed lake it felt as if the water were beading and bouncing off a skillet. Aside from a few boats at least a quarter of a mile away I was completely alone and so, underneath a great overpass, I swam for the next twenty minutes, paddling about in circles like a slightly retarded puppy dog. It was not until I saw a couple of teenage boys whooping loudly as they descended the slope in that gloriously confident manner they are so noted for that I decided to end my own swimming experience and begin the trek back to the car.

The coolness of the swim stayed with me for the next two hours and, to my great surprise the tree at the site kept things rather comfortable until the late day breezes took over the job. It was unnaturally quiet in the campground and I had no company but the flies until around 7:30 pm.

It is the great joy of my life to like my daughters and their mates. While I think there is something contrary to species survival and unnatural for us not to *love* our off-spring, I know too many people who do not like or respect their children, for the child will not satisfactorily comply with their own will and desires. And, while I can see my girls' faults clearer than my own (of course!) it does not preclude me from appreciating what fine, loving people they are. To that end, it was a great pleasure to spend time with Rachael and Andrew, sharing our views about the meaning of life over a fine rib eye that had been perfectly prepared by Andrew on an open campfire. Yes, we did make a fire when the sun went down and loved every ridiculous moment, including capping off the meal with that culinary sticky favorite, s'mores. Any other time I would have considered the gooey melted marshmallow and dark chocolate square on a graham cracker sandwich downright icky, but not this weekend. Also, they went surprisingly well with the right shiraz…

Earlier in the evening when they had first arrived, Andrew had paced about the site with intense concentration, intermittently looking up in order to maximize the broadness of the sky as well as encompass areas he wanted to explore and photograph. Finally satisfied with his chosen spot he had painstakingly sat up the complicated apparitional equipment. Now that dinner was finished and the sky sufficiently blackened, the quantity and quality of celestial bodies were astounding to behold. It had been so long since I'd last reveled in

the mysteries of the heavens and, with Andrew as such a learned, patient teacher, Rachael and I were amazed at the clarity with which we could see Neptune and its four moons.
Rachael and Andrew had had a long hard week of work, as well as having sat in the bumper to bumper traffic from San Francisco to Lake Sonoma, so they begged off further socialization for the evening and retired to the back bedroom, which I had cozened up for them before they had arrived.

"Nay Mah Ee, Nay Mah!" 'A beautiful girl like no other' is what the words to the song meant in my language. Around and around their campfire I danced, holding hands with the Bulgarians from San Francisco. Rhythmically we bounced together as they smiled welcomingly and secretively to me. My broad, grateful and happy face opened by the light from the fire, I tried hard to pay attention to the steps I was being taught while being completely swept away in the foreign, ethereal nature of the experience. So sensual, so evocative! I probably should have told Rachael and Andrew I was going over to the site approximately 150 yards from our own, but my wine enhanced state of euphoria drew me in the direction of the

music and then pushed me to the outskirts of the large group to observe them. Having been spotted, I had been quickly incorporated into their glorious celebration of life. So achingly beautiful and joyous was the sight of them all in camaraderie by the light of the ever growing flames!
It was hard to say goodbye, but I did so within the half hour and after thanking them profusely, scurried back to The Nest for a delicious night's sleep.

The next day was chocked full. It started with a hearty breakfast of steak and eggs with jalapeno cheese, onions and mushrooms and French toast made from the previous night's left over baguette after which Rachael cracked the whip and, less than enthusiastically, we headed out on a hike. By ten a.m. the sun goaded us mercilessly, betting we could not find the lake as we meandered through small pathways in what we hoped was the right direction. Eventually we came out on the main road, halfway between the campground and Lake Sonoma. Curses! Like a scene out of an old western, we crawled through the desert (on the road of course) back to the campground; eagerly hopping in the car and zipping down to the cool sweet reward that had eluded us during the hike.

That night, with our very own in-residence Carl Sagan on sky watch, Andrew spoke with the awe and reverence of an enlightened man on a topic that is, for scientists, the core of their spirituality. He and I followed The Great Pleasure Seeker, Rachael, blissfully into the wild abandon of 'no dinner tonight' - going directly to smores n'shiraz, and, by the light of the stars and our waning campfire, we three made one of life's delicious memories.

On Sunday I made the decision to stay until Monday, rather than fight traffic back through San Francisco and into Anthony Chabot outside of Oakland. Additionally, the heat did not seem as oppressive to me. We three lazed about all morning, yesterday's hike having been enough exercise to last us for the next week. It was close to noon when a young woman in the ranger's vehicle drove up and got out.

"Hello!" I rose lazily and walked toward her, hoping there was no problem.

"Good morning," she responded pleasantly. "Is everything o.k. here?"

"Oh, yes indeed. As a matter of fact, I was going to go down to the front office to register for another night, if that's o.k."

"Well, why don't I save you the trip." She

took out a clipboard from the front seat of the truck that held the required form.

"Thanks." When she had pen in hand and appeared ready I started, "The name is 'Chesbro'."

"Not related to George, the author, by any chance?" She looked up.

"Yes," I said, always so pleased to meet someone familiar with his work. "I'm his wife."

"Really?! He is one of my favorite authors of all time!" Her enthusiasm made my throat tighten.

I wonder if she knew. "He died in November."

"I heard. I'm so sorry."

It was very comforting to receive condolences from a fan. I had always been conscientious about responding to letters, cards, and emails - just as George had been when he was alive. "Thank you. I keep a collection of all of his works with me. Is there any novel in particular you'd like to have that you haven't yet read?"

Her response was immediate. "I haven't read *Chant, Silent Killer*."

The Chant series of three novels is extremely difficult to find in first edition paperback. They had an interesting history. Bantam Books commissioned George to begin writing a series under the pen name of

David Cross. The plan was that after the first three paperbacks Bantam would hire other, lesser known authors to continue the works. The premise of the book was about a modern day mercenary and was to be specifically geared for young men. Bantam was not pleased with the first *Chant*, calling it 'too literary' and had asked George to rewrite it. George balked and, although he got his way, the series did not take off the way Bantam had hoped, but Chant was one of those interesting characters that actors looked at often to option for a movie. Strangely enough, it was mature women who found the series exciting. George could write some pretty dark shit, which was quite surprising considering how much of a pacifist he was.

"I'll be right back, Sherry," I said reading her name tag. I smiled warmly at her before hustling into The Nest.

While Rachael and Andrew gave her the necessary information to complete the registration, along with a ten dollar bill, I pulled the Chant she'd asked for from the shelf and wrote on the front page:

Dear Sherry - I'm so happy you enjoy George's storytelling as much as I always have! Affectionately, Robin

It always felt some how strange but right to inscribe George's books. People who received them from me seemed to be pleased about it so I had continued the practice.

Sherry was delighted to receive the book and we hugged our good-bye before she hopped back into the truck and pulled away. Rachael patted my shoulder, knowing these encounters were bittersweet for me. I sighed deeply and we returned back to the sweet shade for a while longer before they packed up and headed back to San Francisco.

Chapter Nine

They say, "Some days you eat the bear and some days the bear eats you." Monday the bear ate me - before breakfast, even. I could not find my driver's license. It was my own fault, as I remember tucking it and a ten dollar bill into 'the sisters' of my bathing suit before locking the car and heading down to Lake Sonoma on Friday afternoon. I'm afraid the girls are not as perky as they used to be and a bob or two in the lake would have been enough to loosen the whole business. I stopped at the two-man office at the entrance of the parking lot to the lake to see if, by any slim chance, someone had found and turned in my license there. No such luck, but while speaking with the husband and wife team that worked there I learned that they were employed for one month at a time in different federal parks around the country which worked out beautifully since they wanted to travel full time, living in their RV like me. Having piqued my interest, they gave me information so that I might look into it in the future. Additionally, they said there was a wonderful group of full time RVers that belonged to an organization called 'Escapees' and that it would behoove me to

look into it on-line. We exchanged phone numbers and, most importantly, they told me they would contact me should my license turn up. Fat chance, I thought, imagining that my smiling face on the front of the photo ID was probably looking up at the little fishes' bellies by now.
Sometime after having passed Santa Rosa I heard the shower door come down. I had pulled over to the side of the road as soon as I could and hustled back to the bathroom, disgusted with what I saw. The glass was hanging precariously within the broken frame about six inches off the floor. Had the frame given way any further the entire glass would have broken into smithereens - taking out heavens knows what else with it. I bolstered the mess up as best as I could with towels and the rug before calling my new best friend, Jen, at Albany RV. This disaster was not in parallel with my lost license, as Jen directed me to at a wonderful RV service center in San Palo and again, within two hours, I was back on the road headed toward Anthony Chabot.

Poor Janet! What could be worse than working in customer service for a bureaucracy and having your hands tied? She tried valiantly to put me into the Department of Motor Vehicles system for

handling lost licenses but there was no protocol for my particular miseries - that being no internet service and completely across the country. In the end it was her sheer will and determination to offer Real Service to a Real Person that saved me. I hustled my passport, marriage license and the additional paperwork she required off to Rachael's office, where Rachael met me outside the building with a copy of downloaded form MV44. After filling out MV44, copies of all the paperwork were made by Rachael while I waited in the 'no parking zone'. Then I zipped the whole stack, Express Mail, out to Janet's attention. Within two days Rachael would download and print out a copy of my license, which Janet would email me. Lastly, a new license would be waiting for me when I got back to New York for Leah's shower. Thank you, Janet and Rachael!
Ok - so 'some days you eat the bear and some days the bear eats you' is a bit dramatic, but at the end of the day, I certainly appreciated being back amongst the warm, shaggy trees of Anthony Chabot.

Aside from being available for Rachael's day surgery which was two days away, there was one more thing I wished to do before leaving California. I don't know why I was nervous, but after perseverating about it for half the morning, I capitulated to my deeper desire and dialed their number.

"You have reached The House of The Rosary. This is Father Del Rosario speaking. If you wish to speak with anyone else in the parish please leave a message and your number. If not then forever hold your peace." Carl Del Rosario had a wry sense of humor.

"Hi, guys. It's Robin Chesbro. I'm in California, not far from you. Give me a call back when you get in." I left my number after the message before hanging up.

Almost immediately my phone rang.

"Robin!" Janie's voice, in that delicious Hawaiian sing song, was easy to identify. "I just walked in the door from my ukulele lesson and caught the tail end of your message. Where are you?"

I told Janie I was in Anthony Chabot and asked if they had any time to see me.

Moss could never grow under Janie and Carl's feet. Despite being in their eighties, they are two of the most active people I know.

"How about we come over now?"

"That would be great!" I told her, happy to feel I meant it.

*

"George, let me come in!" I pleaded in front

of the door to the men's bathroom somewhere in the miles of maze that was Tokyo's subway system.
"No, I'm fine." He sounded winded but, as always, stubborn.
I sat back down on the bench and waited. Patiently. Trains came. People rushed out of the opened doors and scurried in all directions. Others rushed by me into the open doors as if sucked in by a vacuum. The trains went. The vendor selling newspapers at the little stand was looking over at me more often now. I went back to the bathroom's hall.
"George, is there anything I can get you?" I hoped dialogue would prove fruitful. At least give me an idea as to what I should do.
"No."
"O.k. I'm right here if you need me."
He did not respond.
I sat back down.
A tiny old woman, hunched over and downtrodden, came with her water pail, mop, and cleaning supplies. She entered the men's room. George did not come out. Twenty minutes later the woman came out. She looked up at me with troubled eyes as she passed.
Just as I was beginning to wonder how I would go about contacting the police George came out of the bathroom. His jeans were

completely soaked. Obviously he had taken them off and washed them in the sink. I had never seen his face so abjectly red. His eyes were bloodshot and his hair was plastered to his head. "My Love!" I ran to him and wrapped my arms around him fiercely, never having seen my big ox of a man so compromised. "Are you alright?"

"I am now," he assured me, but then added quickly, "I don't want to go to Kabuki but I want you to go." We were about a five minute walk from the theater which had been our destination when we'd left the hotel, some two hours ago.

"No, No!" I protested. "I want to go back to the hotel. You need to rest!"

He was adamant. "Listen, I'd *never* forgive myself if we'd come this far and you didn't get to Kabuki. You *must* go. Do it for me."

Still I was shaking my head, horrified. "No, George. It's too late - see?" I showed him my watch. It was going to start in ten minutes.

"We can make it," he insisted.

I knew what I was up against and capitulated to his will.

George was determined to forge ahead, but he was frightened at the same time that this episode would recur. This fear exacerbated his roiled intestines and many a side jaunt was predicated on him being able to have one eye on a nearby bathroom.

The air quality of Bejing, especially, was so bad that several fellow travelers in our group were coming down with breathing related illnesses. George seemed easily winded and, over the last two weeks of the trip especially, he seemed to be having more panic attacks. If a lot of walking was involved an intermittent short rest on a bench and, of course a cigarette, seemed all he needed before he was able to continue on. So what if he was slower than everyone else on the bus? We had made lots of good friends, including Janie and Carl, and everyone, even Shu our guide, loved Sweet George and never made him feel like he was holding everyone up.

Although we had looked forward to our three weeks in Japan and China, George had always been anxious about leaving The Hudson and I wondered if his neurosis weren't finally beginning to hamper his ability to travel. Japan and China was a wonderful trip, but it was our last of its kind.

*

Janie and Carl looked the same. Aside from a little extra weight, I was willing to bet they looked the same as they did in their wedding photo. There's something to be said for picking the right parents. "You guys look great!" I gushed, so glad to see them; so

grateful they came.
"You, too, girl." Janie returned the compliment, her broad face glowing with eyes so dancingly wide they reminded me of Dora's from the children's cartoon *Dora The Explorer.*
Carl gave me a hearty bear hug and a loving smile before sitting down on the couch. I sat across from them both on the kitchen booth.
"We were so sorry to hear about George," Janie told me, straightforward as always.
"Thanks." I was 'so sorry', too.
"I hear you have a wedding coming up." I wasn't sure which daughter or when, but I'd remembered the event and did not wish to speak further on the topic of being 'so sorry'.
"Yep. Kahlealah. Next month on the beach. It should be a hoot!" Janie answered happily. Janie did the talking for Carl and herself. He'd always seemed quite pleased with the arrangement.
"That's great."
"How about lunch? Did you eat?" She quizzed me.
"Not yet, but I've got tons of food here. What would you like?" I started rattling off all the food choices I had and was willing to make for the three of us.
They - Janie - wouldn't hear of it. "Forget it. There's a great Chinese food place in

town. You like 'Chinese'?"
You'd think they only had one day to live, the way they packed everything into a twenty-four hour period!
I had to laugh. "Janie, we ate Chinese food for breakfast, lunch, and dinner for three weeks straight in China, remember? Honestly, I haven't eaten it since, but you know what, that sounds great. Let's do it!"
I gave them a quick tour of The Nest before grabbing my pocketbook.
Locking up behind me, Janie gave the orders. "I'll go with you, Robin, and Carl, you follow us."
Carl nodded in agreement and we three went about the business of getting ourselves to the restaurant.
Janie was right. The restaurant she recommended was great. Simple ambiance. Fabulous, fresh food. Between bites of moo shoo pork I asked, "Have you heard from the Zuver's?" Mary and Bob were another couple we had traveled through China with.
"Oh, yeah. We email all the time. They're in Michigan now and are going to their winter home in the Carolinas at the end of November."
"That's great. Give them my best when you speak to them next."
"You give them your best. I'll give you their email address."

I nodded. It would be good to get in touch with them. "I think I'll get in touch with Syd, too."
"How's she doing?"
"Honestly, I don't know. I haven't kept up with anyone, but she'd been hocking me to come to Florida and after I get back to New York I think I'll contact her and make plans."
"Good for you!"
On and on we chatted about the people we'd stayed in touch with as well as snickered in reminiscence about those we'd opted not to. We talked about The Great Wall of China our Yangtze cruise, the rains we'd experienced in Singapore and, when the terra cotta warriors of Xian was brought up it reminded me, sorrowfully, of George.
"You know, in retrospect I'm lucky I didn't lose George right there in Xian."
They both nodded solemnly, probably remembering that George and I finally boarded the bus with Shu close to twenty minutes after everyone else was already on.
"That was probably the beginning."
Again they sat quietly.
"We had no idea what was happening to George. We just thought it was the air quality that made him winded."
"Half the bus was sick by then," Carl kindly offered.

"Isn't that the truth!" I said, glad for the small opening to get off the topic. "Remember that pill from New York? A sore throat was the only thing that finally shut her up!"

We all laughed remembering The Beauty, as George had referred to her.

Janie had ordered enough food for the three of us to feed a small village. While it was being wrapped up 'to go' we had our picture taken by the waitress.

That night as the warm fragrance of eucalypti swirled gently around me I mused on the visit with Janie and Carl, glad I had contacted them. While I had been afraid it would be too painful to see them there was another part of me, with a stronger drive, that needed to accept the comfort offered from those with whom George and I had shared a joyous life experience. I still couldn't talk too much about it, but I recognized that I wanted to.

George, in the form of a full moon once again, beamed down upon me

Chapter Ten

Even though my tongue was slightly blistered and puckered from eating too many salty snacks and two Bloody Marys and I was parked in a Walmart parking lot listening to the howling winds sweep across the desert in Willamucca I was happy. I'd driven seven and a half hours. Greta Garmin had been true to her prediction. The Sierra Nevada Mountains were steep and rugged but in comparison to the mountainous region of Banff they were mere hills. I'd passed eighteen wheelers struggling to maintain fifty miles per hour as if they were sitting still. The real challenge had been the wind. At sixty miles per hour The Nest pulled sharply reacting wildly to the wind's pressure. It was best to remain loose rather than fight with the steering wheel and vigilance had been constant throughout the entire day's drive. I'd circumvented Reno, uninterested in gambling or sightseeing and stopping only for gas before continuing, anxious to cover as much ground as possible in the day. I wondered if the high wind was normal for this time of year or an aberration for the desert, as well as how much longer in the five and a half hours I had left to travel before reaching Boise I would have to endure the difficult driving. But, I was happy. In two days, Friday at 2:15 p.m., I would meet George's son, Mark, for the first time.

We had been writing sporadically for the past eleven years but since his father died Mark had been sending me weekly missives. The day George died I had contacted the prison where Mark was incarcerated. In turn, a pastor from the prison spoke with Mark and then Mark was given permission to call me at which point we cried and commiserated for the allotted ten minutes. Since that communication, Mark had been transferred from Oklahoma back to his home state, Idaho. He was in confinement so while I had been given permission to see him, the meeting would be on a closed circuit TV and we would speak by telephone. I didn't care. I'd happily take what I could get.

At the rate I'd been traveling I'd reach Boise by mid day on Wednesday. Mark's mother, George's first wife, Donna, lived about a half of an hour from the prison. I thought long and hard about going to her home and introducing myself. I'd heard stories from George and later, Donna herself, that their five year relationship had been fraught with inappropriate disturbances on both their parts. Now married for the past 35 years to Bill, Donna seemed, at least during our phone conversations over the past few months, stable and happy. I decided to sleep on it and drifted contentedly into what would be an excellent night's sleep by 8:30 p.m.

The next morning I woke, refreshed and gassed up and on the road by 9:30. A completely open flat road stretched ahead, the winds no longer following me as I headed toward the Idaho border.

"Bill?" I asked, assuming the male's voice that answered the phone was Donna's husband.

"Yes," came the wary response.

I didn't keep him in suspense. "This is Robin Chesbro, George's wife. I'm coming to Boise to meet Mark on Friday and I was wondering if I might stop by to meet you and Donna since I'll be in the area this afternoon."

"Donna's not here - she's visiting with a girl friend this morning, but I think that'd be great!"

His enthusiasm made me feel easier about the possible imposition. "I'm driving an RV, Bill, so I'll set myself up at a campground close to the prison and then I'll drive over."

"No, no." Bill spoke with authority. "There's nothing over there but desert. You come to our house and then we'll figure out what to do with the camper."

"That's awfully nice of you, Bill. We'll play it by ear, then. I have your address so I'm looking forward to meeting you later today, after all these years of talking over the phone!"

He laughed easily. "Me, too. Drive carefully and we'll see you later."

I hung up the phone feeling certain I would be welcome. Hey, stranger things happened in life and this just felt right to me.

I knew that Donna and George barely tolerated each other over the past forty five years for the sake of Mark and once, some twenty years earlier, George had come out to Boise to see Mark. The one and only time. George had told me that he met Bill and thought him to be a very nice guy and that they'd gotten along very well. He had also told me that he knew Mark was deeply troubled at that time and could not imagine him continuing to live the way he was without repercussions from the law. It broke George's heart to see Mark suffering with a bi-polar disorder, unmedicated except for what he was illegally getting on the streets. It took Boise eight more years after George's last visit with his son to catch up with Mark and incarcerate him with five consecutive sentences; the judge using words like 'sociopath' and 'narcissist'. Since then Mark had been on carefully monitored medication. Both George and I had felt that if The State had not stepped in Mark would have killed himself and/or someone else. His letters which had been filled with rage and omnipotence in the beginning years had become more lucid, reasonable, and reflective as his state of mind changed. In the past two years he wrote about the positive, happy occurrences in his life, as he began teaching remedial math to other inmates and taking courses himself. Since he was back to playing the guitar in an inmate rock and roll band and belonged to a softball team, we would sometimes refer to prison as Camp Scuffy.

Despite the obvious successes Mark was enjoying, George was adamant about never returning to Boise. He hadn't been very negative about his last experience but he did say that since his last name was Chesbro he might be opening a door to scrutiny by the local, Boise police. George was nothing if not antiauthoritarian and paranoid, but he reminded me that even paranoids had real enemies and had remained steadfast in his determination never to go there again.

The day's ride included a dusting of snow as I passed over the border between Nevada and Idaho and, carefully monitoring both the road's grade and speed limits, I arrived at a Walmart less than a mile from Donna and Bill's house at 3:00 p.m. While Bill had been generous of spirit regarding my impromptu visit, I would not take for granted that Donna would feel the same so I called the house, hoping to speak with her directly. I was not disappointed. Her voice, never above a gentle, feminine whisper was distinctive. Too bad I'd heard so many stories of the painful treatment each had visited upon the other. Partial to my George, of course, I'd developed a bad habit of wincing when I heard her voice on the phone, as he was never happy to hear from her even though she always called regarding Mark. Also, he did not share her view of Mark having been unfairly treated by the court system. Surely they had both protected themselves by fortifying their psyches with rewritten memories over the years.

"I'm at the Walmart on Main." I told Donna. "Would you and Bill like to come here for h'orsderves and drinks?"

"First of all, we don't drink."

Oops, I'd forgotten the two of them decided to give that vice up many years ago.

"But, anyway, we'd like you to come here. You can park the motorhome in the front of the house."

"Are you sure, Donna? I don't want to impose and it's not like I gave you any notice..." my voice trailed.

"I'm sure. Bill told me you were coming and we've been expecting you."

"O.k." I said. "I'll be there in five minutes."

Closer to fifteen, I arrived at their home, a small one story house centered on a well-manicured piece of property. I circled the charming development in order to situate The Nest closer to the curb and away from a large tree with overhanging branches. By the time I turned off the engine Bill and Donna had come out of their house and were standing on their front porch.

"In for a penny, in for a pound." I thought to myself and took a deep breath for energy to meet the situation.

I exited The Nest with a big smile, determined that the 'kick off' should run smoothly. Bill, lanky with an easy going charm, took long strides and met me almost curbside. Donna, a tiny, handsome woman with long gray hair had to walk double time and even at that she joined us after Bill had already given me a great bear hug.

"It's great to finally meet you, both," I

relaxed, realizing that statement was true. It felt good to put faces to the names and voices and, for better and for worse, they were part of George's past.

I was quickly escorted up the walkway and into their home. The living room contained the usual prerequisite pieces of American living furnishings and included an inordinate amount of personal pictures from chair railing height to almost the ceiling on every wall. I sat on the couch and Donna, eager to speak, stated matter-of-factly in her throaty whisper, "I was talking to my girlfriend earlier and said, 'God! My ex-husband's wife is coming here later today, I wonder what the fuck she wants.'

O.k. So this wasn't what I expected to hear. Since I'd just sat down, standing up and exiting in a huff like an English Lord seemed, minimally not my style and maximally, untenable. I whisked around inside my head searching for an appropriate response. Nothing came to me so I reiterated my itinerary. "Well, I have an appointment to see Mark on Friday afternoon at 2:15 and since the trip from San Francisco went much quicker than I'd expected, I thought I would drop by to meet you."

She eyed me suspiciously and then, satisfied, launched in another direction.

"You got through to someone at the prison? I've been calling all day to find out when you could go and no one has called me back. They never call back."

"I called two weeks ago to find out what days and times I could see him, and then again two days ago, just to make sure of the procedure and days. I'd been approved two months ago and maybe since they had me on their list as coming in from out of state it was easier for me to make arrangements."

"That's probably it." Donna muttered, still annoyed at the lack of respect she felt she was receiving from the prison personnel. She rose gracefully from the couch and, in what can only be described as a complete change in demeanor she asked, "Would you care for a cup of coffee?"

I wasn't too interested in coffee, but I wanted her to know I appreciated the gesture. "I'd love one," I answered smiling.

As Donna left the room Bill got down to business. "Do you have a gun?"

I was of two minds before answering the question. First of all, I don't want anyone to know what I do and do not have. Let them worry, if they're the type that should. On the other hand, I don't. "No. I'm figuring you're asking because you think I should have one?"

"Of course! You have a right to protect

yourself."
"Well, I didn't grow up with them so, frankly, they seem scary. Also, there are plenty of stories about people getting shot with their own gun…"
"Idiots who aren't committed to using them. If you are gonna have a gun then you've got to know you can use it if someone means to do you harm."
"You know, I can totally envision myself shooting someone coming into my RV. And not in the knee, either, I don't mean to be sued down the road." I liked Bill and, as a natural result, could feel myself comfortably starting to pace; picking up idiomatic expressions, accent and tone. "The problem is I don't even know how to use a gun. Never even held one!"
"Hell, my son Billy and me go into the dessert all the time to shoot off rounds. When I was a kid we shot snakes all the time."
Ethnocentrism came to mind. Different cultures. Different mores. Bill was just trying to see that I was protected. I tried to see his point of view. "Well, if you grew up with them and you're used to them then that makes it comfortable."
"Right. C'me here." Bill got up from the barcalounger and headed toward the back room. I rose and followed him.

“The problem is,” he started by taking out a dark grey metallic gun with a long barrel that looked suspiciously like a six year old cowboy’s weapon, “that since the government can’t stop the sale of guns they are makin’ it difficult to get the ammunition.” He did a little clicking thing with the gun before handing it over to me to hold. I assumed he had made it child proof for me, but I didn’t take any chances and pointed the weapon to a corner of the room. It was heavy and that’s how I knew it didn’t belong to the cowboy. “This is *very* nice,” I said hoping to convey the right amount of gravitas for a prized item I knew nothing about.

“Sure, it is! And look over here.”

I looked up from the weapon in my hand to see Bill holding a *real* cowboy’s weapon in an old brown leather belt with little loops for bullets. It was plenty dusty. Bill gave it a shake and a swipe with his hand before passing the whole business over.

While I looked at the ancient piece in the gunslinger’s holstered belt Bill told me proudly, “That was my dad’s gun.”

“It’s beautiful, Bill!” I was pretty awed by now.

“Sure it is!” He supported my enthusiasm. “Looka these…” his great hand spread upward to a glass enclosed case on the wall.

These are real collectors."

I looked at each one intensely, wondering which would be best for me when I heard Donna's voice down the hall. "Show her my snub nose," she'd added to the conversation.

Obediently, Bill left the small den and crossed the hall to their bedroom. I could hear a drawer open, and figured it was probably in the end table. *My* end table held tissues, reading glasses, a crossword puzzle book, and, of late, a dildo since George had abandoned me and Mr. Peju was not readily available.

Bill came into the room with a small shiny silver number. The handle was pearlized. It was lightweight and seemed to me to be a 'reasonable' weapon. "This is great!" I hollered in the general direction of the kitchen, which was unnecessary as Donna had entered the den at that moment, two coffee cups in hand.

"Yeah, I'm happy to have it," she assured me as she handed me the white mug with painted roses.

"Good." I exchanged the gun for the coffee and nodded my approval for both.

She eyed me again suspiciously before deciding to tell me a story. "About three months ago when Bill was trucking – mostly he's retired now – there were some

Mexicans coming up my front walk. I got my gun and waited by the window to see what they would do. They just left after a couple of minutes, but I was real glad I had that gun then!"

The world can be plenty tough for people, I know that, but I'd never had the kind of experience Donna was talking about. "I'll bet!" I'd said, imagining myself pretty wide-eyed from her point of view. I tried to overlook her description of the possible perpetrators as being 'Mexican'. Maybe they were and maybe they weren't – hell, they probably were the woman was not blind, but I just hated *that* being the description. It would have been better if she'd said they were two seedy characters looking mischievous, but I guessed that would have been pretty naïve of me.

"Yeah, well, look here's a picture of my Billy." Donna's graveled voice softened noticeably as her attention shifted to the pictures on the wall opposite the gun case. "Here's him in The Navy," she pointed with her free hand to a young man in full dress uniform.

"Very handsome," I assured her. "How long ago was this?"

"Oh, lemme see, he's 37 now, so fifteen years or so."

I nodded, imagining what he might look like

now.
"And here's my daughter, Karen. She lives in Ohio."
A good looking young girl in an '80 mullet hairdo smiled at me. I smiled back.
"Yeah, well, she has two kids and I don't see her. She was from my third husband."
I knew Donna was married before George but hadn't realized she'd been married after George and before Bill. "Pretty," I said groping for an observation and response as the girl now seemed almost ghostlike, any personality disappearing into the faux wood wall of the den.
"Yeah, well, her father was a real holy roller. *That* didn't last too long." Her lips pursed in sour memory.
I nodded my head with an empathy that stemmed from my well of 'general compassion for others'.
Donna, once again, changed her disposition and cheerily told me, "I got four kids from four husbands. My motto is 'one to a customer'."
"That's a good one, Donna!" I laughed pretty heartily before including Bill in the conversation, "And you saved the best for last!"
Bill beamed.
"You got that right," Donna said as the three of us exited the tiny room.

Both walls of the long, dark hall were also covered with family pictures. Most were of Billy. "Got any pictures of Mark?" I asked. "Oh, sure!" She said happy to comply. Once back in the living room we approached a wall of obviously older pictures. A young boy with his older sister was pointed out for me. "Here's Mark with Michaele. He was about seven years old."

I moved in close, eager to see what the man I would meet in two days looked like as a child. "This was when you lived in Seattle?"

"Yep, before I met Bill."

I tried to recall the time line as recited to me by George but it was a little fuzzy. "So then you moved out here when Mark was in high school?"

"Right. That's when he started with the crystal meth. I was working nights as a bar tender and didn't know he was sniffing glue and other shit since he was, like, ten or eleven."

"Yeah – and she wouldn't let me discipline him, either," Bill chimed in. "He coulda used a heavy hand now and then to keep him in line…"

"Hey, nobody hits my kid but me!"

"George said you were really good to Mark," I offered, hoping Bill might feel he'd done his best for a teen that was already

deeply troubled.
"George? Don't get me started on what I think about George! What we could have done with some *real* money from him. Hell, Bill and me lived in a trailer no bigger than yours with three kids for close to ten years before we could afford to buy this place!"
I was silent for a moment trying to process what I'd just heard. I knew George sent money every month for Mark and Michaele, which I thought was damned good of him considering she ran off with the kids after the New York courts had given him full custody. She obviously thought he should have given more. She obviously thought he *had* more to give. I kept my voice low and thoughtful. "Donna, George was as poor as a church mouse. He didn't have any money at all." A sad but perfect example came to mind. "When we got together he was gluing a tooth back in his mouth with crazy glue 'cause he couldn't afford a dentist!"
This was obviously a new bit of information for Donna as her eyes widened noticeably. "Whaddaya mean? He was a big writer!"
I laughed at the common misconception. "Yeah, well, he wrote two dozen books and tons of short stories, but he barely, and I mean *barely*, made a living at it. Plenty of times he had to go back to work at Rockland Psychiatric Center as a teacher because he

didn't have enough to pay the bills. Honestly, he just wanted to live as a writer."

"A writer! I wouldn't read anything of his. We had two little kids and all he wanted to do before and after teaching all day was *write*."

"That's true," I said sadly. "George hid out from the world by creating little worlds he could control. He had his demons, you know."

"Well, I'll be damned! And here I am thinkin' he's thinkin' he's better than me! He was always looking down his nose at me.

I nodded my head sympathetically, unwilling to address that comment.

"Well, I'll be damned…"

I guess it warranted being said again.

"How about you guys come over and see my RV?" I thought the timing was good for me to show off The Nest.

"Great!" said Bill enthusiastically.

Donna was noticeably quiet as we traipsed across their front lawn. Arriving at the front steps first I unlocked the door and we three went inside.

Bill had a million questions for me. Like most men, three quarters were about what sources of power it had. "And, look here, Donna, she's got a full working kitchen!"

"Oh, sure," I told them easily, "I cook all my own meals. I prefer my own cooking to

eating out."
"Yeah," Bill smirked at Donna sarcastically adding, "Just like you!"
"I don't like my kitchen messed up," Donna retorted, probably for the thousandth time.
I knew kitchens weren't used the way they used to be, especially for women who'd had day jobs most of their lives. Before I could actually think my next thought through it came out of my mouth. "I've got a nice rib eye and some tilapia - how about coming back in about an hour and I'll make us all dinner?"
They were hesitant in responding.
"I also make a hell of a focaccia bread," I proudly enticed them both.
"Sure, why not!" Donna finally answered.
As they descended the steps of The Nest we made a time to meet back for dinner. Bill, checking my tow bar connection, told me to be careful I didn't run down my battery on Maxine and, then moving to the rear of the car, advised me that the back tires were cupped – I'd probably need a rear alignment. I gratefully made note of both observations. Donna said she collected New York license plates and I told her that as soon as I was done with my travels she could have them.
As I set the table and happily bustled around the kitchen preparing our meal I couldn't help but giggle. This was going wonderfully

well. I could just imagine George saying, "Only my Robin could pull this off!" On a more serious note it occurred to me that meeting with Donna was very healing for her. Maybe I had more information she would find of value…

It was about three in the morning when I heard the banging. I could hear the male voices in a Spanish accent. They were laughing, too, like a kind of weird, drug induced laughter. One was saying, "See if you can find the handle, man, find the handle!" In a sleep-induced stupor I tried to wake myself. What was happening? The little window next to my bedside was open and I thought I saw one young man banging on my front door. The other one must have been to his right side and out of my sight. Mother of Fucking Christ, they were trying to get in! I grabbed my cell phone off the end table and, by the whitish dim light that came down through the opaque plastic dome in the bathroom created by the moon I dialed 911.

"911 - What is your emergency?" The trained professional asked me.

Shakily and whispering I told her, "I am in an RV, alone, and two men are trying to get in."

"Where are you?"

Thank God I remembered the address – I gave it to her.
"Do they have weapons?"
"I don't know – I can't see too well." I tried to peak out my little window. "Should I turn on a light?"
"No. Try not to let them know you are there. Do you have a weapon?"
"No." I thought about the fire extinguisher under the sink in the bathroom and, in stealth mode, I took it out."
"Are you in a safe place?"
Very quietly I carried the fire extinguisher back into the bedroom and crawled back into bed, cowering in the corner. "Yes."
"Can you describe them for me?"
Wide awake now, I carefully looked out my little window. The banging and talking had stopped. Where I'd previously seen the young man I could now see only a large shrub rustling with the night breezes on the street corner. Straining my ears I heard no one. "I think they are gone."
"The police will be there shortly," she assured me.
"Wait – stay on the phone with me 'til they get here!" I begged, uncertain they wouldn't return.
"I will," she said.
"How will I know it's the police?" I asked her, a new fear cropping up.

"They will identify themselves."
That seemed a little sketchy to me, but I figured I could check them out through the kitchen window. I didn't have long to wait.
"O.k. they are here now," I heard myself say to the woman on the other end. I could see clearly that the two men were, indeed, police. "Thank you so very much." I told her gratefully.
"You're welcome." She added, "You have a good evening."
Shakily laughing with relief I assured her I would now.
The police had arrived within seven minutes of the call, I had figured. They asked for a description but, while I wanted to be helpful, I truly could be certain of nothing. They also asked if I thought the two men meant me harm or if it was just mischief. Interesting question. Upon a brief contemplation I realized it was just mischief. They probably were walking around stoned and came upon the RV. The novelty of a big tin can in the middle of the little development most likely piqued their interest, but they may have quickly tired of the knocking game and just moved on. I voiced my thoughts to the police. Yes, probably just mischief, they agreed.
Despite the trauma, the first of its kind for me ever, I fell back asleep about an hour

later, which I thought was pretty good.

The next morning Donna came out to the RV at 8 a.m. to let me know that their son, Billy, had returned from his night job as a trucker. She wanted me to meet him, as well as to offer me a cup of coffee.

Although I didn't want to upset her I knew I had to tell her what had happened outside their home during the night. Wide eyed and visibly upset, Donna scurried back in the house while I threw on a shift and then joined them in the house, eager to meet Mark's stepbrother.

The front door was open and since I knew they were expecting me I walked in. I could see from the look on Bill's face he'd already heard the news.

"Time to clean out the neighborhood!" he said tersely through pursed lips.

"Just mischief, Bill, I'm sure. I think drugs and mischief."

A man who has guns to protect himself does not consider mischief a viable reason for disturbing one's night's sleep.

"You must be Billy!" I moved on enthusiastically, walking toward the dark, good looking man next to Bill.

He was a little shy to my forthrightness and, considering everything he'd been hearing from his mother and father about the unusual meeting between the three of us,

I'm sure he was plenty skeptical. Hell, I'd have been if I hadn't experienced it, myself!
"Nice to meet you," he said politely.
Donna came out of the kitchen. "Bill and I are going to take you to Idaho City today for sightseeing. It's really interesting – one of the largest mines in the west most people don't know much about it. Then we're going to take you out for early dinner at one of the best places."
"Donna!" I was taken aback by her generosity. "That is so nice of you, but really, you don't need to entertain me. I'm very happy right here."
"Nope. We want to. Least we can do after that dinner last night - and we haven't been out there ourselves in a while. It'll do us good."
I couldn't think of one reason not to take them up on the offer so I graciously accepted.
Then Donna added, "And I'm going to take you to the prison myself, tomorrow. I know right where to go."
I had really wanted to see Mark alone and was concerned Donna was going to take advantage of being with and out of town visitor to spend time with Mark, as well as monitor our conversation. Also, my time was extremely limited; a mere forty-five minutes.

This worry was unfounded as she followed up her offer with, "I'll just wait in the car and read my book 'til you're done."
"That's very kind of you." It would be great not to have to take Maxine off the back of The Nest. "Thank you!" I added earnestly.
Donna's thoughts turned as she told me about her children. "Billy lives across the street, two houses down. He usually stops by on his way home from work for breakfast. Michaele is working at an adult living center – she lives with Billy and when she comes home tonight she's looking forward to meeting you. Bill's son, Steven'll be by to pick up his car this morning – he drives a school bus. You'll meet him in about an hour."
"Sounds great!" I was beginning to realize that Donna and Bill had created a very close knit, loving family of his, hers, and theirs. It felt wonderful to be so welcomed. I also thought sadly about poor Mark missing all of this.
Bill and Billy started heading towards the kitchen.
"I don't want you guys making a mess!" Donna hollered after them, certain her words were falling on deaf ears.
"How about you all come over to the RV and I'll make bacon and eggs?" I offered.
Bill didn't hesitate long. "You got some of

that focaccia left?"
"You bet!"
"Billy, you're gonna love this bread," he assured his son.
Billy, obviously used to his parents' ways, shrugged in happy resignation as if to say, 'whatever' before adding, "I'm going home to shower. I'll meet you back here."
"O.k.," I answered, even though he was talking to his mom. "Come right to the RV!" I was eager to show off The Nest again.

Chapter Eleven

"There's no doubt about it," I told Donna and Bill. "Steven has 'the curse'."

A retired pilot in the US Air Force, Bill's son had been married six times and was now with a wonderful woman who, despite his track record, wanted to marry him. Everybody in the family loved her. He loved her, too. Personally, I thought it was a good thing he wasn't a woman – unable to say 'no' he'd have spent most his life pregnant! And it wasn't as if he was trying to set any records; he was just in love and if that was what his intended wanted then he was happy to give it to her, despite the fact that the 'happy ending' had always eluded him.

I saw the look of fear on their faces. "Don't misunderstand me," I quickly assured them. "I'm not talking about the curse of having been *married* so many times. Oh, no, no. I'm talking about the curse of being unbelievably charismatic and handsome! *All* the women must want him." I, myself, having briefly entertained what having sex with this young stud muffin might have been like, whimpered openly to Donna and Bill, "I assure you both that I don't *want* to be a

cougar, but I could definitely see why some women do!"
On a more philosophical note I added, "Anyway, we've all got a different path to live. His is just kind of interesting…"
Donna shook my reverie by introducing her brother's life into the conversation. "Andy was a real heartbreaker, too. The women flocked to him."
I'd heard plenty about RandyAndy, as George called him - like he was a small time porn star. Like Andy had Mark mule for him as a drug carrier when he was a teenager and that George blamed Andy for Mark ending up in the garbage can. I didn't say any of that. Instead I said, "You know what George told me? He told me that if Andy ever showed up at our door I was to hide in the bedroom immediately, because no woman could resist him! I told him, 'Are you *kidding* me? What am I, some kid? Someone who isn't completely and totally in love with you that you should think I'm so easily swayed??' But he was adamant. He made me swear. What a riot – that George sure had his paranoia!"
"No," Bill spoke earnestly. "George was right. Andy had this unbelievable way with women. When he died I had to destroy boxes and boxes of video between him and all of these women."

Donna chimed in, vehemently. "I told him that someday some woman's man was going to get him. He just laughed at me, but I was right!"
I'd heard that, too. "You know, Donna, I don't think this kind of extreme behavior comes from nowhere. I wouldn't be surprised if your brother had been sexually abused as a child."
Donna got real quiet. I was sorry to have upset her, but the whole topic was crazy with 'upset'.
"We both were." Her voice was surprisingly matter of fact.
It seemed to make a lot of sense out of a life that had, long ago been fraught with chaos.
"I'm sorry to hear that, Donna."
"I can't believe I'm telling you this!"
"Hey, why not? This is real life shit."
"Yeah, it is…"
"Look," Bill took one hand off the steering wheel and pointed at a sign on the side of the road that read,

Idaho City, Idaho
Over ten thousand ounces of gold mined here!

There is something about driving along, chatting with people. Maybe it's the lack of eye contact and we just get comfortable with other human voices. Maybe it's the time element. Whatever the mechanism at play, we let our guard down and I was happy for it. "This is great!" I said to no one in particular as we continued driving through the little city.

"Oh, you're '*Joy*', alright." Donna laughed at me.

"Whaddaya mean?" I didn't get the joke.

"Well, many years ago – when you and George started dating – George told me he'd finally found joy in his life. I used to ask Mark, 'How's your father and 'Joy' doing?' Mark'd be annoyed with me. "Don't say that, mom!' " Donna mimicked him, "'One of these days I'm gonna make a mistake and call Robin 'Joy' by accident.' "

I had to admit that was pretty funny. "Donna, you're a riot!"

"Yeah, I'm a riot alright. You know something – I'm not angry at George any more. It's all gone – every bit. All those years. All that anger. Gone."

"Good for you!" I was pretty impressed. As far as I was concerned, that was quick processing of new information. Donna sure was a smart cookie.

We drove around the small town and, as advertised, had a terrific, home cooked meal at a local restaurant. We all split a humongous piece of lemon meringue pie, most of which was wrapped up and brought home for Bill to have for a midnight snack. There was no lack for conversation.

Once back home, we all walked over to Billy's house. According to Donna, he had wanted to tidy up before showing me his home. There I met Michaele, Donna's oldest daughter from her first marriage who George had adopted. Proud for having been off crystal meth herself for the past six years, I was shocked at the toll it had taken on her physically. She, through all her harsh life experiences, had become one of the most compassionate, loving people one could hope to meet and, considering George's emotional abandonment of her as well, I was truly touched by the warm, enveloping way in which she welcomed me. She didn't have to but she did.

I was getting the nickel tour of Billy's living room when the phone rang. It was Mark!

Since Mark occasionally received an opportunity to make a phone call when he was out of his cell for one hour each day, he had decided to speak with his brother Billy. He had no idea I was in town or, for that matter, would be coming to see him tomorrow. Additionally, he certainly would have no inkling to the fact that I was in his brother's living room, schmoozing it up with all his family members! Quietly I motioned for Billy to give me the phone when he was

done speaking with Mark. A few short minutes later the cordless was passed to me.
"Mark!"
"Yeah?" His voice was wary.
"You'll never guess who this is!" I was brimming with giggle, but did a good job suppressing it.
There was silence on the other line.
"It's JOY from New York!" I exclaimed.
There was no response.
"It's Robin! I've gotten permission to see you tomorrow at 2:15! I'm here with everyone and we're having the best time! I can't wait to see you!"
He was obviously in shock. I could almost imagine him trying to make sense of everything he was hearing. "Tomorrow? You're coming tomorrow? Robin? What are you doing at Billy's house?"
"I got here yesterday. Everyone has been so kind to me, Mark. It's been wonderful." I knew his time on the phone was very limited. "Here's your mom. I'll see you tomorrow!" I handed the phone to Donna.
Joy, indeed.

*

"I see spiders in their webs, but I'm not taking any stock tips from them." George told me this while making little dismissive swipes with his hand. It was his way of letting me know he was having mild

hallucinations.
"O.k., George." I spoke assuring. "I'll get the nurse and we'll see what's going on."
We had been in the emergency room for quite a while. Everyone had been attentive, as is usually the case when a congestive heart failure patient arrives via ambulance. While blood work was still being cultivated, it was obvious from his fever that George was festering something not easily fended off.
The weird thing was we had been out on the boat the day before, sailed up to Shady Harbor Marina for a lovely breakfast on the veranda, and headed home without so much as a hint of a problem. As a matter of a fact, ever since a MUGA Test revealed George's heart was working at 18% capacity, a combination of heart drugs had brought it up to 32% and we'd had peace of mind that things were headed in the right direction with only a brief set back at which time a defibrillator and biventricular pacemaker was put into his chest. The operation was considered unsuccessful in that there was no vein on his right side to connect. The specialist told us that should his energy level worsen they would perform a more invasive surgery and screw the lead onto the right side, but until such time as it was warranted, the lead had lay unconnected.

But now, whatever it was, had thrown him into the usual symptoms. Difficulty breathing. Low energy. Water retention. I knew we'd been a bear about his eating – salt under 2000 milligrams a day and testing his sugar each morning. The morning routine had also consisted of checking his blood pressure and weighing in. If he gained two pounds it was a dangerous sign that water was beginning to build up. We'd been able to live our usual active lives for one and a half years since the trip to China. Even the doctor was shocked that we had sex regularly and that his performance was not a problem. As a matter of fact, his cardiologist had said that George was getting more sex than *he* was and threw us out of his office with a laugh and a wave of his hand – pleased his patient had been doing so well.

This business of hallucinations, however, was a complete mystery. I pressed the buzzer again for a nurse.

"Yes, Mrs. Chesbro," the tired young girl answered the call as she opened the curtain to expose us both.

Concerned but pleasant I kept my tone even. "Marlene, George is having mild hallucinations. Do you know what could be causing this?"

She looked up at the wall of numbers, ever

changing. “His oxygen level is dropping – he may need to wear an oxygen mask ‘til it comes up. A bed has become available on the heart floor. We’ll be moving him up soon.”

I knew what soon meant. Soon meant ‘not never – but not soon’.

A strange looking man; tall with a pinched face, thick large glasses and a determined, serious demeanor joined the party. He wasted no time with pleasantries, but I saw from his name tag that he was an infectious disease doctor.

“Mr. Chesbro?” He addressed the patient.

George nodded.

“I’m Dr. Peter Mangiorri. Do you have any aches in your joints? Any swelling?

George shook his head.

“What medications are you on?”

George looked at me. I rattled them off.

The strange looking doctor bobbed his head in comprehension, taking them all into consideration before asking, “Have you been bitten by a deer tick recently?”

Chrissake. Would we even know? Dr. Mangiorri started looking over George’s mostly exposed body and there, on the inside of his wrist, he spotted a red, slightly swollen area. “That’s it,” he finalized his diagnosis, “You have Lyme’s Disease.”

As quickly as he had come into the room Dr.

Mangiorri exited. Twenty-five minutes later George was on an intravenous drip.

By eight p.m. we were ushered into a room on the heart ward. I'd made it my business to know a lot of nurses on the ward from our last visit and hoped to see a familiar face this time. The nurse assigned to George was not one of them.

"Go home," George kept saying. "Go home and take care of the puppies."

It was close to ten. I'd been there since eight in the morning. The poor dogs! "O.k., my love, I'll go home now and come back early tomorrow morning. I'll get a neighbor to watch the dogs tomorrow."

I hated to leave him. He hated for me to go. I told the nurse, "George's oxygen is low. He's been hallucinating a bit. Call me anytime if there is a problem. I'm twenty minutes away."

She nodded agreeably.

The nurse who called me at six a.m. was not as agreeable. "Mrs. Chesbro, how soon can you get here?"

"What's happening?" I asked still half asleep.

"George has become unruly. He's ripped out his IV and has been trying to leave the hospital. We've had to tie him into his chair."

I was wide awake now. "Are you fucking

kidding me?" Was what I wanted to say, furious they had obviously not addressed his oxygen issue regarding hallucinations. Furious they had waited so long to call me. Furious my poor George had to go through this crap to start with.

"I'll be right there," was what I said instead.

George, convinced he was being held captive in Abbu Grave, was pretending to be asleep. He wasted no time addressing me when I came in the room. His eyes were wild with fear and paranoia. In a terse whisper he congratulated me on getting through the enemy lines, and together we plotted our escape.

It took the better part of the day to bring him around mentally, and the better part of the next two weeks to stabilize his system. Additionally, while we were in the hospital he was forced to go on dialysis because of all the intravenous he'd been put on. He swore like a sailor. He told me he was not going to live like a goldfish. He said 'never again' to dialysis.

I didn't leave his side. After that experience I knew I never would.

*

I wonder how many people have ever been to a prison. Considering the United States has over eight million of its citizens incarcerated, the largest of any country -

third world or otherwise on the planet - you'd have thought most of us would have visited someone at least once. This was my first time. Donna knew everyone there.
As we entered the maximum security facility of Idaho State, a brand new building to accommodate the ever growing numbers, Donna smiled brightly hoping the employees would reciprocate. Some did, some didn't. For my part, it appeared to be a typical bureaucracy. I signed in. The tightlipped blonde behind the front desk asked for ID. She compared signatures. She told me why I would not be seeing Mark at 2:15, but that I may see him at 2:45 for my allotted forty minutes. I told her that was fine. I sat down and waited. And watched. Donna kept me amused with little stories about past experiences, good and bad, she'd had with the guards. I nodded, more in appreciation for the diversion than the actual stories, which were just to let me know she'd put in her time here.
I watched. Did I say that? Yes. I watched all of the family members and all of the friends that came and went through that system that hour on that day. Everyone was emotionally contained, even though some were more overtly pleasant than others, looking around and smiling. Some had bad manners, bad mannerly children, bad

hygiene, and bad dispositions, but most were well-scrubbed and decent looking people. Moms and dads came with looks of shame on their faces. Others looked defiant and annoyed. I wondered what their stories were. Had they 'done their best' or was Joey 'just a bad seed?' In the end, we all had one thing in common. We all deliberately wanted to be with another human being that had defied society so badly that they were in a maximum security prison. I even spent a few moments pretending I wasn't like everyone else. Feeling like an outsider helped me withdraw from actual participation, since I was uncomfortable with the game I was participating in…

I was called to the security desk at 2:45. By 2:46 I was in a large cafeteria-like room. The room contained many tables and chairs, as if set up for a chess tournament – minus the chess sets, of course. The two long walls of the rectangle room were lit up with bright colored, inviting food vending machines. The prisoners and their guests were able to dine on whatever the twenty dollars in change permitted into the room with the visitor could buy. Rules and rules and rules were a good way to keep the masses in conformity - and an obvious necessity.

I was directed to the short wall of the room. Unlike the movies where the visitor would sit on a chair facing a glass partition and talk on a phone, this wall held many television monitors. I was instructed to sit in front of a specific monitor and when the television came on I would be looking at Mark and he would be looking at me; until that happened I was staring at a reflection of myself. Further, I'd been instructed to use the telephone on my right to speak with him when the connection was made. I was giddy with excitement until I realized that I hadn't prepared anything to discuss. Before I could make a plan the television screen brightened and there I was, seeing Mark for the first time.

When my daughter, Rachael, was born the strangest instinct took over. I memorized her face and body, instantly and intensely, so that I would be able to identify her in the future. Seeing Mark was a little like that experience. I searched his face, swiftly and deeply, looking for signs of George in him. They were there. The television monitor was of poor quality, but it forced me to look even closer at George's son. Mark was in his mid forties, shaven bald and overweight. His face, broad and open, reminded me more of George's father than George, but his nose and his eyes were his father's. Mark, too, was scanning my face. I hoped he saw love. I was brimming with emotion when our eyes locked.

"Hello, Robin," He found his voice and spoke first.

"Oh, Mark! It's so good to finally meet you!" All of the years of writing so freely had not prepared me for the attachment I'd felt toward him that moment.

"I'm so sorry we have to meet this way."

"I'm not. I'm happy for whatever I can get. I am just so very, very glad to see you."

"I can't believe you came here."

"I told you I would." It was true. In our letters since his dad had died I told Mark that sometime I would come out to see him. I just hadn't known when.

We continued to look at each other's faces, soaking in as much information as we could about each other with our eyes. I said, "Your mom has been great. Everyone's been great to me since I got here!"

He seemed pleased, but said, "I'm so glad my dad had you, Robin. Sometimes I would think how much alike he and I were. Being loners and all. I'm glad that in the end you were with him."

"Thank you, Mark. I loved him very much. He loved you very much, too. No matter what had happened with you he used to say to me, 'Mark has the kindest heart.'"

"I like to think I got that from him. I just wished I'd had some of his talents!"
"He was proud of you, Mark. Between teaching remedial math to other inmates and taking classes while you're here gives you a life experience you just wouldn't have had on the outside!"
"I know. I was a mess."
"How are you feeling?" The question was about his physical health.
"Better. After they popped all the blisters on my right lung when it collapsed last year they told me I had blisters on the left, but they aren't going to operate until it collapses."
"What a strange thing to have happened!"
He smiled sadly. "Not really, Robin. The blisters came from all the crystal meth I took. Basically, I've got the body of an unhealthy 70 year old."
I thought of his step-sister, Michaele, and nodded thoughtfully. "I'm so sorry, Mark. You know, your dad self-medicated with alcohol. The doctor said it was his drinking that weakened his heart muscle. It's so damned common to handle our life that way."
"Yeah, I guess we shared that weakness. I'll tell you the truth, after twelve years of being in here I *still* have the taste for it. I think if I got out tomorrow I'd want it."

"No kidding! Your dad had his demons, too. You know, he was a bit of an obsessive compulsive." That was the kind of thing I could say face to face with Mark but not get into in a letter.

"Yeah, I'm a bit of a germaphobe, myself. I don't like anybody getting to close to me, either."

I noticed he had a glove on the hand he was holding the telephone with. I nodded.

We sat quiet for a minute.

"I'm glad we had a lot in common. Dad and me. It makes me feel not so alienated from everyone else in the world to know I had him in my corner."

I knew what he meant. His father was a decent man with an odd working brain. "I think we all needed to feel connected in the loneness of living, no matter what our circumstance." I hoped that helped him feel not so alone.

"What are you doing with your days?" I asked him.

"Well, I don't know when they are going to let me out of confinement. Of all the stupid things to get into a fight before you came here! So, I get one hour a day 'out' to take care of anything I need to; like taking a shower or making a phone call. Once I'm in the general populace again I'll be able to meet visitors in the room where you are now and have more time to exercise. Hopefully get back to my classes."

"I hope so, too, Mark."

The screen went blank. The phone went dead. The visit was over.

I sat there for several minutes trying to take in what had just happened. No warning. No goodbyes. No nothing. Unceremoniously shut down. Self-consciously, I got up and headed out of the room. Once in the hall the tears rolled down my cheeks. I guessed everyone was pretty used to seeing that scene, so I didn't feel too bad about the public display. I mean, I wasn't bawling or anything. Donna was waiting for me outside.

"How'd it go," she asked kindly.

"O.k." I mumbled. "It was great to see him, just disappointing at the end. And it was so short!"

We were about half way home when Donna said, "I want to take you to my brother's house. It's not far."

I was not sure why, but if it was something she wanted to do then I didn't mind. "O.k., sure," I told her.

She began the story. "This past March I was watching the local news on TV in the morning and I heard them say 'a man stabbed multiple times' and 'Cleary Blvd.' I knew immediately it was Andy. There was no doubt in my mind. I threw on some clothes and came over here as fast as I could."

We were driving into a senior complex. There were many trailers in the park, all well kept and decent looking. She stopped in front of one that was boarded up and put the car in 'park'. "The cops were all over the place. I told them I was his sister. At least I got inside the house to get the jewelry out and all the boxes of porno. Then I raced to the hospital. He was a mess; looked like shit – twenty-two stab wounds. They'd given him something for the pain and when he saw me he wanted to speak to me. I bent down and he told me he was sorry for everything, but I told him there was nothing to be sorry about." She became silent, stuck back in that moment of extreme privacy between the two of them, moments before he died.

"I called the two girls I knew he'd been with most recently and told them to come and get their shit and their porno. Most of the other women were scattered to the winds, so Bill and I just burned the tapes out back of our house as fast as we could. You could see the smoke for miles – lucky somebody didn't call the cops on us."

I definitely lead a sheltered life. I'm pretty

certain my eyes must have been wide as saucerss. I kept quiet.

Donna continued. "Once the cops found out who did it – some bimbo's husband - I went to every single house on this block. I had to tell all the people here that this was not a random murder. That my brother had been killed for personal reasons."

"That must have been tough, Donna."

"Yeah, it was. 'Humiliating' is more the word."

"See the porch?" She continued, pointing to the side of the trailer. "That's where he got him first. Then Andy must've tried to get into the house, but the bastard followed him into the living room, stabbing and stabbing him, and that's where he left him, like an animal, to die."

"Chrissake, Donna."

"Yeah, Chrissake. And you know what gets me?" The question was rhetorical. "He always, *always* used to tell me how I had to protect myself. Back in my whoring around days when I was a bartender he'd given me a pick so sharp you could pierce wood with it. He told me to keep it under the bar. Any woman who'd be thinking I was with their man'd be in for a world of hurt if they started up with me! I could puncture four tires in twenty seconds flat. I just can't believe Andy didn't have himself covered.

You let your guard down for one minute…" Her voice trailed off, possibly imagining a different outcome. "I told the cops I'd kill the bastard myself, if they let me."
I didn't even bother saying, "Now, Donna, that wouldn't really make you feel any better," because I knew that it would. Vengeance ran strong in the woman.
She put the car into drive and we circled the block before passing the house one more time.
"Donna," I told her, "I'm leaving tomorrow morning. I understand there's some snow expected from the north and west, so I want to get an early start. Maybe I can beat it out. Anyway, I'd like to take you and Bill out for dinner tonight. Billy and Michaele, too, if they can make it."
"Well, they're both working, but dinner sounds great. There's visiting hours tomorrow, too, you know, why don't you stay over another night?"
"No," I told her, although I was slow in saying it. "As much as I'd love to see Mark again, I think we've said what we need to say – for now at least. I'll come back. Definitely I'll come back to see you all again, but I've got to start heading east. My daughter's bridal shower is in three weeks in New York, and I might make a few stops along the way to make." I mused quietly

about the possibility of finessing visits with two of my sisters and a life-long friend on my trek back to the east coast.

"Gottcha. Where do you want to go for dinner?"

"You pick it. I like everything."

Donna decided on Mexican. We had a great time. I went to bed early and woke early, as planned. They both met me at the front door of The Nest to say their good-byes and wish me well. The visit had been absolutely delightful, we all agreed, and after starting up The Nest, I circled their small block and turned onto the main road. As I passed their home on my right they were there, waving goodbye. I honked my horn loudly and waved back, grateful for such a fine, loving experience.

Chapter Twelve

I had figured that five four-hour days of driving would put me at my sister, Margaret's, home in Springfield, Illinois, but with the forecast of snow and general bad weather pending it was my hope to get as far west and south as possible that first day on the road. The flat easy drive through Idaho was made even more agreeable by phone conversations I had with family and friends back in the Albany area.

First I'd wanted to tell George's sister, Judi, that I'd seen Mark and spent time with Donna. Judi hadn't seen Donna since she was a teenager and her one lasting memory was of Donna's brother, Andy. She often recounted how he had almost killed her as he careening south on the New York State Thruway at one hundred miles an hour once - with both Donna and herself in the car. Giving Judi the sordid details of Andy's death, as they had been relayed to me by Donna, was more lascivious than a soap opera.

Since Judi and George were seven years apart they had precious little in common but when we had moved from Nyack to New Baltimore the geographical proximity made it a little easier on Judi and since I was so much more social than George, getting together, however infrequent, was a pleasant, enjoyable encounter. I liked Judi and her husband, Dick, as well as their children and grandchildren, it was just that our bohemian, reclusive life style left little room for others. Judi and I prattled on about the family until we felt we were all caught up with each other. We closed our conversation, as always, with a promise to be in touch soon again.

Next I called my beloved Valerie. I hope that every human being on the planet has one person, not their significant other, that they can share their life with the way I share mine with Valerie. My mother's sister and seven years my senior, we were glued together more with common family history than actual life experiences, but the shapes our lives took as we matured were easily recognizable and empathized by the other. Both blessed and cursed with addictive behaviors, Valerie had successfully learned to live one day at a time and had all of the glorious insight that goes with this formula for success for close to thirty years. She knew the sorrows and pitfalls of life's humiliations that made recounting the story of my time with Mark, Donna, Bill and all of their extended, nuclear family all the more poignant. We spoke of the exhilaration when truth sets us free, healing, forgiveness, and being able to move forward. My great touchstone affirmed my journey whenever I reached out to her and my appreciation for this gift has never faltered.

Happily I drove along, circumventing Salt Lake City and crossing the border into Wyoming. Unlike the QEW through Canada, Routes 84 and 80 had rest stops every 45 minutes or so. It was a joy to refuel, pee, and be on my way so effortlessly.

I made one more telephone call that afternoon to my dear friend, Charlene. As much as I loved hearing her voice it was a difficult call to make. She had ovarian cancer and had been on chemo for over a year without having ever gone into remission. We'd met when George and I first moved to New Baltimore and needed a mechanic for Maxine. Charlene ran the business for her son, Kenny, the mechanic. We liked and trusted them both so much that we bought a truck from them and counted on their expertise as well as fair handedness the entire time we lived there. When I told Charlene about holiday gifts I was getting for the teenage girls at St. Anne's Institute in Albany she was one of the first ones to hop on board, supplying winter gloves for all 150 girls. Openhearted and touched by the sorrow of others, I came to learn that giving is a great part of Charlene's nature and was proud to call her my beloved friend. The conversation, as always, was honest without being maudlin. We spoke of her 'uncomfortable' symptoms, our children, and lastly, my travel. Where I am is always important to Charlene, as she has lived her entire life in Ravena, leaving the area only once to visit her childhood friend who had moved Florida. As always, I told her she was 'in my pocket' as I kept her dear to my heart, wherever I was. I had never met anyone more appreciative for the small joys each day brought to her.

*

Mel wanted George to come into Manhattan for a meeting with a movie producer who was interested in optioning Bone. George hadn't seen Mel in over ten years and that was reason enough to go, but he knew what these meetings would entail. The woman wanted to sit down with George because she could not afford to pay a substantial optioning fee and was hopeful that if she was able to meet George face to face and tell him how much she loved the story and why she would do a great job producing it that George would be moved by her enthusiasm for the project and either accept much less or acquiesce on a fee altogether. Honestly, George would have sold an option on one of his novels for no more than a pack of gum if he thought there was a real possibility that a movie could have been made and although he would often say, "It's not professional if it's not paid for," his fee, like any mid-list author or low end prostitute, was nominal. That sort of arrangement could be made by Mel without George's personal involvement. Despite having told Mel we would meet him the following Wednesday at his offices in midtown, George began grousing almost immediately about leaving The Compound. I made arrangements for us to stay at a nice hotel and ordered opera tickets for LaTraviata, happily chirping about having an 'assignation with my sex slave' in the City. This titillating approach lightened George's spirits about the impending trip, as well as the fact that he wanted Mel and me to meet. He'd always said that if anything ever happened to him I should trust Mel regarding the business of his works, as he had for the past thirty years. Their relationship had never been warm but was professional and despite my years in the business world I felt a bit intimidated by the proposition of a sit down.

The hotel was two blocks from Mel's office.

That was a block and a half too much for George that cold May afternoon. We rested three times along the way, once so he could have a cigarette. Fortunately we waited close to a half of an hour to see Mel, which gave George an opportunity to catch his breath. I must admit I enjoyed watching all of the interesting characters come and go in the reception area.

The walls of Mel's office were bookshelves, from ceiling to floor, filled with best sellers and iconic biographies. People he knew. People he represented. For the first time I did not feel disturbed that Mel hadn't given George's work more attention. He was a very, very busy man. A little schmoozing took place before business, just to warm up the dice so to speak. The producer pled her case. George listened kindly and humbly. He said it sounded wonderful and that the numbers could be worked out between Mel and herself at a later date. I knew what he really wanted. He said, once and very quietly, that he would like to have an opportunity to write the screenplay. Work. He wanted work.

The fumferring started. When a producer is putting together money for a project they are often committed to that money's people for various aspects of the production. Screenwriters were usually one piece of that pie. George would often say that screen play writers fancied themselves as *real* writers and got way too much glory. In defense of screenwriters, everyone knows that novelists tend to get verbose and writing screenplays is a sharp, action-filled art – usually one page per minute of the movie. In George was, however, the exception having successfully written two screen plays for previous works that were extremely well received by the industry.

The fumferring continued. Commitments had obviously been made and I knew George would not say another word on the topic. Gentle and soft spoken - but firm, the author's wife said that writing the screenplay was of *paramount* importance to George. Neither Mel nor the producer could possibly have known why.

*

After having put in close to seven hours of driving, I punched *WalMart* into Greta Garmin. She turned her sand filled hourglass over and over until she came up with an acceptable response to my request. Eleven miles ahead I could get off the main road and be at a WalMart within three minutes. Sweet!

It helped me rest easy to see so many RVs at the parking lot's fringe. I also appreciated having seen signs that the lot was continually monitored not only with cameras, but with security guards circling, as well. The Nest nestled comfortably amongst compatriots and, pleased with the day's travel, I decided to start dinner. I didn't get very far, realizing I'd have to hop into the WalMart to get more angel hair pasta. Just as I was about to leave The Nest the phone rang. I was delighted to hear Donna's voice.

"Hi! We just wanted to know how far you got today."

"I'm in Wyoming!" I happily reported.

"Great. I also wanted to say how terrific it was to meet you and how much Bill and I really enjoyed our time together."

"Me, too, Donna! Oh, and Judi sends her love."

"Back at her. You have a good night's sleep and I'll talk to you soon."

"Thanks, Donna, thanks for everything."

I shut my phone and, locking the door behind me, started walking towards the WalMart. I didn't get far. Stopping dead in my tracks I observed with horror that my New York license plates had been stolen off Maxine.

Miserable and unsure of what course of action I should take, I was no longer interested in dinner. I climbed back into

The Nest and poured myself another drink. Alone with myself once again, I cried angry tears at George for leaving me.

*

It was as funny as it was sad. George and I, sitting in a well-worn wooden booth across from each other at The Tollgate where he and the gang used to hang out when he was in high school. We had just come from Dr. Millora's office where it had been decided that the time had come for George to undergo the more invasive surgery to reconnect the right lead of his pacemaker. Fourteen months after his bout with Lyme's Disease, his energy had begun to seriously wane again. He was grateful there was something else they could do to help him. I was in such good spirits that I suggested we go to The Tollgate for a burger – something that we could comfortably fit into his diet if we were careful for the next few days. George lacked nostalgia, but to satisfy me and because the promise of a burger was irresistible, we went to his old stomping grounds.

"Is this where you used to sit?" I asked him coyly.

"Nah – I sat up there," he pointed to one of the swivel stools at the counter. "Never on the other side, though."

O.k. So the left side of the horseshoe

shaped soda bar was where he and his cronies reigned. An older gentleman and woman came into the soda shop.

"Do you know him?" I asked. Surely George must know everyone.

"Yeah – we called him 'droopy drawers'" he told me, observing the sagging jeans of the unsuspecting classmate. "He was in my third period Algebra."

I giggled. Noticing a large round yellow plastic water cooler had been placed at the entrance of the soda parlor I remarked, "You know, I think it's wonderful that they offer free water at the front door."

George, with his arms crossed on the bench leaned towards me. His blue eyes twinkled with mischief. He smirked widely and, cocking one eyebrow, shared the awful truth. "You think that's a water cooler? It's not. That's the girl's gym uniform!"

I began laughing uncontrollably at the ridiculous image of girls playing field hockey wearing the mustard yellow vats around their torsos. The more I laughed the more George's smirk contorted, his mouth opening and shutting wider, as if his wit amazed even himself. His eyes danced gleefully. My George. My teenage, young stud George, was flirting with me as if he was a senior in high school and I was an impressionable sophomore. Behind the gray-white, wispy hair and the wrinkled face of the old man before me was the impish teenage boy that all the girls in high school had swooned after. I laughed and cried at the same time. Finally finding my voice I'd said, "Oh, George, you slay me!"

*

The next morning I woke to snow. It wasn't much, just flurrying, but it was enough to make me move quickly. The television weathermen had been all over the impending storm as it was abnormally early in the season for such an event. I was probably one of the first ones to leave the WalMart, grateful it wasn't worse and hopeful the front would move slowly since both the bad weather and I were heading in the same direction. Not too far into my morning's drive it caught up with me. Fortunately, there was no wind and I didn't see other big rigs pull off into rest stops so I kept going. I monitored the tires of the semis, telling myself that if any trucker had to stop and put on chains then that would be my cue to stop driving for the day but since the snow was not expected to let up anytime soon stopping wasn't really a viable option unless it became dangerous. I'd only be putting off the inevitable. The flat straight road was a much easier drive than the winding mountainous areas I'd traveled through the past two months and I considered that a tradeoff. I kept at a steady 60 miles an hour. Eventually boredom set in so I turned on the radio for company. My options were country music, country music or country music. In defense of airway freedom there was also charismatic Christian. I chose country music, deciding, resignedly, 'If not now then when?' A couple of catchy tunes offered enough of a distraction to encourage me to keep on pressing forward. As a matter of fact, less than 24 hours of having realized that my license plates had been nipped I was feeling pretty good towards all humanity; in no small thanks to Tim McGraw and a lot of others who obviously had it a whole lot worse than me.

As it had become my habit to read every sign on the road, the large green announcement that we were all officially on The Great Continental Divide enhanced my sense of camaraderie with the truckers. Crossing The Continental Divide in a snow storm – what a deal!

In my side view mirror I could see a large convoy of semis quickly approaching. I was sorry I didn't have a CB and resolved that somewhere in my travels I would pick one up. It would be great to hear about the most recent weather conditions as well as possible traffic jams or accidents up ahead. I kept my speed steady as the first one came alongside for what seemed like an inordinate amount of time.

"Come on, pass, damnit," I thought to myself, uncertain why the trucker didn't keep his 70 mph pace. Eventually he passed and put on his right blinker to indicate he would be pulling in front of me. I clicked my high beams twice to let him know he had enough room to pull in and that I would be monitoring the distance between us. In he came, signaling his thanks to me by putting on his right direction signal, then his left, and finally tapping his breaks three times. Then the next semi came alongside, with the same modus operendi. The first truck pulled up ahead so that the second trucker could pull in front of me. He, too, hit the right direction signal, then left, and then tapped his breaks a few times. That was a little weird. The third, fourth, and fifth trucks followed suit. I was used to them tapping the breaks twice to say 'thanks' but this seemed a bit much. All of a sudden it occurred to me that they were, perhaps, 'winking' at me with their right and left blinkers. Having CBs they probably could see I was traveling alone in bad weather. I didn't feel threatened by the truckers, quite the opposite, it made me laugh and loudly I began to sing along with Josh Turner to my new favorite song, 'Will you GO with meeeee?' Of course, I can't be certain but it made me chortle and I liked thinking it was so.

On and on I pressed along the flat terrain until close to four o'clock at which time I punched WalMart into Greta, hung a Louie, and hunkered down once again cold but satisfied with the day's travel. Out came the bottle of wine. Out came my now weathered and dog eared map of the USA and the yellow highlighter. Tomorrow I would be leaving Wyoming, going through Nebraska, and then Indiana before hitting Illinois. At the rate I'd been moving I could be at Margaret's in two more days travel. I'd have to head south. It was a bit out of my way to see her - if I was pressed for time and looking to make a beeline for New York and Leah's shower but such was not the case. More importantly, Marg had been experiencing a hard go of things and was finding life difficult between her poor health and heavy work load as a chef. She hadn't seen family in a long time and I hadn't seen my niece, Terra or my nephew, William in many years. I pulled Greta off her stand on the dashboard and had her join us at the table. As I looked closely at the map and plugged in a few other addresses the plan began to gel. After visiting Margaret I could continue slightly northeast, stopping at a girlfriend from Junior High School who had become my close pen pal over the last forty years. I had another sister, Julie, and her baby, Genevieve, who I'd only seen twice since she was born. I would love to spend time with them and that wasn't too far out of the way. I traced a path further east and using Greta realized for two hours more travel time I could meet up with Valerie, then easily drop off Mimi's wine, have a visit with my dad, bring in The Nest for a check-up and reach The Sheraton Crossroads – all in time for Leah's shower. Maybe I could see Charlene, too!

It seemed to be a pretty ambitious schedule, but I began to feel more excited about spending time with people than I had in many, many years. I also had to admit that my experiences, first with strangers in Canada, then family, certainly Mark, and yes, even Donna and Bill, were helping me. I realized it was common for people to use other people as welcomed distractions from their pain and this did not necessarily please me, as I considered it a weakness, but it was beginning to dawn on me that the exchanges were almost necessary in order to at least temporarily let go of the nonstop intensity of my pain for it to heal. Kind of like taking a muscle relaxer so that I wasn't always fighting against the contractions of the strain.

I made a couple of calls, asking for flexibility on arrival and departure dates, and was pleasantly surprised at how welcoming all seemed to be.

*

A sea change had come over George. I think it started when we had the garage built next to the house. The winters were brutal and I had lightly said to George there was no reason we should have to shovel out the car and truck every time it snowed. He quietly agreed. The contractor and all his workers were very flattering to our surroundings and this pleased him. Rather than be annoyed at the imposition of people in such close proximity to him every day, George toddled out each morning to chat with the fellows and see what they were up to. They quickly learned he was not checking up on them but was, rather, awed with their talents and pleased to have them there working diligently to enhance his home. For my part, I was downright thrilled to have a cast of hungry men to cook for. They arrived at 7 a.m., in time for breakfast, broke for lunch at 12 p.m., and left for the day at 3:30 p.m. My excuse for all of this cooking in the beginning was that we lived too far away from a place where they could buy lunch. It just snowballed from there.

Additionally, George and I had often toyed with the idea of adding an art studio/guest room and had the perfect spot in mind for it. Our contractor, Duane, agreed and after the garage was completed he drew out the plan, first on a napkin in pencil and later for the town's inspector on a 'nice piece of paper.' We justified the expense saying our savings were just moving from one pocket into another.

Our trust in their talents was not ill-founded. Aside from an excellent reputation in an area he grew up in, Duane kept good relationships and his men were personally fond of him. Duane was a big man, although light on his feet, and he soon began to check on the boys during breakfast and lunch hours. He even started showing up at the ice cream parlor at 3:00, joining George at the counter for whatever late day goodies the ice cream girl had prepared. We told Duane we wanted to have a big cook out for all the fellows and their families after the job was done. Shyly, he said that would be nice. To that end, it was a glorious warm sunny day to give thanks, that Sunday all the boys and their families came to our home. We all played horseshoes by the river's edge and chatted on amiably into the night. George regaled everyone with stories of his wild behaviors in his earlier days, prompting others to share their unlikely high jinks, as well. It was good to see him so happy and energized by all of the testosterone that surrounded him.

Two weeks later, and two days before his second heart surgery, we were scheduled to host a brunch. George and I had committed the previous year – or shall I say I had committed and George had acquiesced – to hosting this brunch for his 50th high school reunion. Despite the fact that George was the class president, his days of being the social butterfly he was in high school had been long burnt out of him. Furthermore, since he was not prone to nostalgia he considered those with a heavy interest in reunions to be living in the past. Since my own high school experience was less than positive I enjoyed the pleasure many of 'the gang' took in planning the big weekend and worked diligently on the committees for both his 40th and 50th reunions. Kindly, they had adopted me as a quasi mascot, and if some took offense to my involvement they didn't voice it out of deference to George.

With the date quickly approaching everyone on the committee scrambled to make the event as fun filled and well organized as possible. George's energy continued to wane but he was determined not to live as a goldfish, so we moved forward with our plans for the brunch and limited our participation in the weekend's events. We would stop by at the VFW on Friday night for an hour or so to meet and greet everyone. I told the gang I had too much cooking to do for Sunday so we would be taking a pass on The Dutch Apple boat ride down The Hudson on Saturday afternoon ("but wave to us as you all go by the house…"). Saturday night the big dinner and dance was to be held at The St. Andrews Club in Albany. George would be giving a speech but we'd leave shortly after that. Sunday would be the brunch.

I was amazed at the energy level George possessed that weekend. He was downright ebullient; seeing and speaking with as many of his classmates as he could. Everyone seemed to love George. He'd obviously gotten along with jocks and eggheads alike and he thought all were more talented and smarter than he.

Not wanting anyone to consider me a trophy wife I'd joked, "The *second wife* is the trophy wife," before adding in a faux serious voice, "The *third wife* is The First Grade Teacher!"

*

I really liked Marg's kids. Terra had, through sheer determination and student loans, put herself through college and at the tender age of 24 owned her own home and taught junior high school English. I was certain that William who was equally bright but not as ambitious would eventually find his way. He was living with Terra and working in the kitchen of a local restaurant. Their company, together with Marg's when she wasn't at work, filled me with good spirits and hopes that their life's path would not be as difficult as Marg's had been. The fact that Terra and William shared my philosophical views about human nature added to a sense of camaraderie that I greatly appreciated but rarely came across.

Since I was settled in one spot for at least a few days I decided it was time to contact the authorities at The Department of Motor Vehicles regarding my stolen license plates. I was advised that I needed to file a police report and send all necessary paperwork to their offices. I felt much more sanguine about the procedure than when I'd lost my license and the bureaucracy didn't bother me a lick.

My call to the local police netted immediate results. The sheriff already knew I was parked in Terra's driveway and said he would be there in five minutes. Jokingly, I asked him to make it ten as I was not yet dressed for the day.

A tall beefy blonde man who took his duty seriously questioned me in detail as we sat at the kitchen table in The Nest. I think he was rather pleased with the prospect of 'going national' as he put the license plate information into the system, eagerly assuring me that if the plates showed up *anywhere* in the USA they would be quickly recovered. He suggested we check to see if there had been any damage to the car; a thought that had not occurred to me. Upon closer inspection I could see, for the first time, that the nuts and bolts had rusted completely shut to each other and that the only way the license plates could have been taken off was to cut around each bolt individually. As proof, there was a little bit of the blue and white plate beneath each nut and in front of the corresponding bolt. This had to have taken a lot of time.

We spoke of my suspicions and, feeling comfortable in giving personal advice, he'd said he was surprised I went to see Mark in prison in the first place and didn't think *he'd* do it. That gave me pause. Certainly I would never deliberately put myself in harm's way but meeting George's son had felt important to me.

I realized that's why the sheriff was a sheriff

and I was, at least temporarily, a nomad.
I told the sheriff how long I would be parked in Terra's driveway and gave him the nickel tour of The Nest I was pretty sure he wanted.
That Friday night I went to my first local bar as Marg and Terra's guest. I enjoyed observing the camaraderie between them and all of their friends in the close quarters of the tiny dark place that represented to me every tiny dark local bar across America.
The next morning it was time to go. For the short time I spent with my sweet sister and her small brood they were delicious company. I happily drove off after reciting my new mantra, "Company and fish are alike in that they start to smell bad after a few days."

Staying with my pen pal, Linda, and her family concerned me a bit more. Although I always preferred my own bed and would sleep in The Nest, I didn't really know Linda very well. Let me rephrase that. I knew Linda on a *very* personal level; that of sharing oneself without boundaries through the medium of writing letters. No eye contact, no immediate feedback to our words, we wrote introspectively, as if in dialogue with ourselves. We had only gotten together three or four times in the past forty years and our lives were, for all intense and purposes, polar opposites. Linda and Bob were social people who enjoyed family, church, community and vacations at Disney. I could be considered to be something of a spunky cowgirl in contrast; especially since George and I had got together as he reveled in and encouraged my dark humor which was not always the epitome of social grace.

To Linda's great dismay and my sheer unadulterated joy, her children were extremely bright free thinking cowboys and cowgirl. There were three. Matthew, the eldest, was for the most part self taught. A minority by birth, he had been adopted as a newborn by Linda and Bob back in the 80's. My daughter, Rachael, who was four at the time, was deeply impressed with the tremendous amount of love and gratitude she felt emanating from them and, despite the difficulties in adopting a Cabbage Patch Doll back in those days she got *her* wish immediately; a black Cabbage Patch Doll. Matthew was certainly quite smart but unfocused. His life experiences and political views were varied and extreme. Many a letter from Linda had been fraught with fears and concerns for him. Since my mind's eye conjured up pictures of Linda as a teenager; a tall lanky, freckled faced redhead with a high pitched voice, it was hard to imagine her trying to wrangle a big dark male. But wrangle she did. Bob, also fair and soft spoken, never wavered in his love and respect for Matthew which was a fact not lost on Matthew.

Dinner conversation proved to be stimulating and, despite my not knowing Matthew well, I held his feet to the fire for every comment he made, demanding he back it up with fact and logic. I recommended he read *Civilization and Its Discontents* by Freud. He was pleased as punch with the exchange. Linda and Bob would probably have preferred quiet digestive time at the table but they were gracious about the intellectual bantering.

Their second child, a son born to them shortly after Matthew's adoption, was not living with them at the time. Rory was attending college in Florida. After bouts of melancholy he had found his way clear to strike out on his own and leave the nuclear family behind. No small accomplishment. George had met Rory and considered him, as he considered my sister Marg's son, William, to be 'alternate personalities'. That meant they wouldn't be taking a job at IBM. Rory would find his way in love and accomplishments on the road less traveled and, as far as I was concerned, that was the good news. Bob and Linda tried not to be overly solicitous and remained cautiously optimistic. I made sure they both knew I considered inner strength to be manifest in those times you feel fear but move ahead anyway and that I had a lot of respect for Rory.

Linda and Bob also had a daughter, Marilyn. Fair and sweet, Marilyn was as tender of temperament as her parents. She studied anthropology and sociology at Ohio State in Akron and lived home, nestled comfortably with her parents. A gentle soul, I enjoyed listening to her recount her studies and offer opinions in the quiet, unthreatening setting of the living room sofa. She had been Salutatorian of her high school and enjoyed acting and, despite serious health issues, never complained.

Each day I walked with whoever was available through the many acres of unfarmed land that had originally belonged to Linda's grandparents. I met her cousin, Gregor, who was married with two children and lived down the street on another piece of family property. I told Linda I was happy to have met him after all these years, especially since I happened to know she'd had a grand crush on him as a teenager. Reminding her of this made her blush terrifically and made us both aware of the secrets in our hearts we carried about the other, endearing us further.

*

Dr. Millora was thrilled. The operation was a success without any complication. They were able to screw the second lead of the bi-ventricular pacemaker to his right ventricle without the use of his veins. George was in recovery an hour before I had been previously told he would be. They did, however, want him to be on dialysis a few hours each day during his hospital stay just to give the organs a chance to rest while he recuperated. He happily complied. Although he developed a sore spot on his backside the nurses showed me how to apply the ointment. This little insult made him pout. He sniffed, saying from that moment forward he was no longer going to wear any clothes at all; he would walk around naked wearing nothing but a Davie Crocket raccoon-skin cap on his head. Leah, having used her vacation time to fly in and assess the house and help me with the physical therapy, said she was going to buy him one for Christmas.

He returned home within the week, weak as a kitten but pleased as punch with the hope of renewed energy. I purchased a white plastic chair to put in the bathtub downstairs so that he could sit while I washed him. He wasn't very pleased. I told Leah I'd paid too

much for it. She told me to 'get over it' because I'd need it again in the future. I wasn't very pleased.
A month later we returned to the surgeon's office for a checkup. An x-ray of George's chest showed that his lungs were clear and the doctor happily told us both that George could resume normal activities.
The following day George left The Compound to vote for The President of The United States.
The next day we made love.
The day after that he went back on the treadmill for fifteen minutes.
A week later he came down with flu-like symptoms.

*

Oh, how I just *loved* that little Genevieve! My most beloved sister, Julie, and her doting husband, Geza, were the luckiest parents in the world! As far as I was concerned, that little one put the Gerber Baby to shame with her brilliant sparkling eyes and angelic demeanor. Every little twist of her bow-shaped mouth and wrinkle of her furrowed brow made *me* gurgle with delight. Babies are a salve for a wounded soul.

*

The new receptionist at Dr. Millora's office was a pain in the ass.

"We *usually* schedule an appointment for the patient to come in and see the doctor," she'd told me haughtily.

"*We* usually ask Dr. Millora if he *wants* George to come in or if he *prefers* George to stay at home," I responded snarkily.

Dr. Millora returned my call promptly, as always. "It sounds like a virus. Call me if anything changes - like if he gets a fever."

George was satisfied knowing Dr. Millora had been advised of his symptoms but that he wouldn't have to brave the cold weather for a half hour trip to his office. His blood pressure was fine, no water retention, his sugar was normal.

George moaned. He loved to moan. He told me that was part of being sick – being able to moan. Kind of like a bonus.

"Oh, *brother*," I told him rolling my eyes.

"Oooohhhhhhhhhhh!" He moaned louder for my attentions, lowering his mischievous eyes.

We both laughed. But he had it bad.

He insisted on going up and down the stairs, following his daily regimen. His appetite was fair; depending on whether I'd made him macaroni and cheese and if there was any more Mayan chocolate ice cream.

Can't you just sit still? I'd demanded, watching him slowly navigate the stairs.

"Ooohhhhhhhhhhh!" He groaned back at

me.
Three days later he thought I should call Dr. Millora again.
I sighed. "O.k." I'd told him. "Let me check your blood pressure again, just so I have some numbers to give him."
I put the blood pressure cuff on his thin arm. It read of 75 over 35. I thought the cuff was broken. I tried it on myself. Normal reading. I tried it on George again, being careful of the placement. 75 over 35. I called Dr. Millora's office. A different doctor, one George and I didn't know, called me back.
"Dr. Millora is away. George needs to go to the hospital." The stranger told me in a cold and calm voice.
"He's due for medicine to lower his blood pressure, perhaps I just won't give it to him?" I asked hopefully. My ignorance of body mechanics was glaringly inadequate.
His flat affect did not waver. "No, he needs to go to the hospital."
"O.k." I meekly answered and hung up the phone. I thought of calling back and demanding that Dr. Millora be advised of the situation, as he had told George and me many times to insist on speaking with him if we felt we needed to. I dialed "911" instead.

Back in the emergency room once again, George and I made ourselves comfortable in our little cocoon-like enclosure.

"It's not my heart. It's not my lungs. It's not my kidneys," he told me sadly. "It's Me. It's systemic. I can feel it. I'm dying."

Ever the thespian. "Don't be so dramatic!" I insisted, kissing his hand.

He took off his watch and gave it to me to hold. I put it on my own wrist.

They sent him for a chest x-ray. He had pneumonia. Could be viral. Could be bacterial. Bacteria they could fight. Viral he would have to fight on his own. Nonetheless, they made up an antibiotic cocktail that went into his IV drip. We transferred to ICU.

The nephrologists said dialysis.

George, discouraged but hopeful, agreed.

Twenty minutes later one of the nurses hurriedly entered the ICU waiting room, waiving for me to come with her back to his room.

"He's giving us a hard time," the nurse hurriedly told me. "He's confused. When we laid him down to prepare for dialysis his oxygen and blood pressure plummeted again. We're trying to force oxygen into his lungs through the bi-pap, but he's fighting us."

Once inside I could see George was

struggling to take the mask off.

"He's not confused," I answered terse and frightened, "He doesn't want it."

I ran to his side and grabbed his hand in mine. "Please, George, let them try to rest your organs so that you can fight this."

"No," he shook his head vehemently, demanding to be understood through the plastic. "I don't want it."

George and I had a little visualization we used with each other to give the other energy when we were low. I put one hand on my heart and my other hand over his heart, sending light. He pushed it away. I saw him close his mouth, trying to hold his breath.

The pulmonologist came into the room. "He needs to be intubated. *Now*."

I was whisked out of the room. The sense of urgency was overpowering.

*

The weather had turned viciously, unpredictably, unseasonably cold. Each night I had been determined to sleep in The Nest, but was galled as I watched other RVer's put on their blinkers to head south off Route 80. They were heading for warmer climes. I was still heading east to New York for the shower.

"Only for the love of my Leah," I cursed softly under my breath.

I stopped to pick up lightweight metallic insulation for the windows of the RV. Cutting the right sizes and laying it up under the window shades I began to feel like I was living in the center of a baked potato. I pressed on, aware of the fact that it had been close to a month since I'd needed to stay in an RV campground, only using a dumpsite for my black and gray water tanks every other week.

It was grand, as always, to spend time with Valerie and her wonderful husband, Jerry. To say that their gracious, warm styles made me feel welcome is an understatement and does disservice to the intensity of their openheartedness. I knew that no matter what horrors might befall me in my life I could count on a roof over my head, food in my mouth, and clothes on my back with them. They are *that* generous of spirit.
Mimi came by to pick up her stash of wine. I could feel our time together had changed the nature of our relationship and was grateful we'd both had that time to share.
It was all swell.
It was all wonderful.
Restlessly, I took to the cockpit and headed upstate.
A pattern had begun to develop.
As happy as I was to share with the beloveds

of my life, every single time I got back on the road I cried. Hard, long cries. It wasn't that I wanted to stay longer with them and certainly I was looking forward to the next encounter on my agenda, but as I drove it came. Torrentially. Snuffling, blubbering, *driving*, wiping my eyes and blowing my nose, *driving* and eventually ebbing into little whimpers. *Driving.* Forget about texting and talking on the phone. There should be a law stating you cannot *cry* and drive.

The time I was spending with people was just a dam, holding back my pain of loss until I was alone to release it.

Once upstate I visited with Charlene. There is nothing more worthy in this life than understanding the essence of Appreciation and she had it. We replenished our aching hearts using each other gratefully, and then I got back on the road again.

The Nest was tended to at Albany RV. Maxine got a check up and new tires. I did not drive by our home on The Hudson.

I saw some of George's classmates.

I met up with Dick and Judi.

I spent time with my dad again and, since I was using his address as my home base, I went through my mail. Amongst the profferings was a little 'love note' from Mr. Peju, hoping that I would return to the winery some time soon. On the front page of the pamphlet was a picture of him sitting proudly with his pretty wife and two lovely-looking daughters. I sighed and laughed. Oh, well, the fantasy had served me just fine at the time…

It was all swell.

It was all wonderful.

I drove back downstate for the shower.

*

George's children, his stories, were neatly arranged in the order in which they had been written on an end table aside his bed. Wagner's *The Ring* played softly as Rodney and Piggie Boi sat atop the cassette deck. Making room for all of this was no easy task considering the wires and connectors that ran like a rat's maze around, into, and out of George. I wanted the lights bright enough for me to read to him, but not glaring down on us both. Curtain shut, please. I made sure that all of the staff knew - as they prodded, poked, turned, and drained George's orifices - that this was a great man deserving of their respect. He was not just a body.

Everyone was wonderful. Yes, please. No, thank you.

George had been intubated. It meant he was in a semi-coma state. As the great machine pumped air into his lungs he could rest without struggling for breath. Dialysis would rest his kidneys. They did everything they could to alleviate all stresses, allowing his body to fight the pneumonia.

Dr. Millora came, assuring me there was good reason for hope. The fact that George may or may not *like* being intubated was too damned bad. Into each life a little rain must fall. They needed to be sure they'd done all they could. I needed to know I'd given him every chance.

The pulmonologist guaranteed me that people on their sure death bed walked out of ICU and people who seemed to have excellent chances did not. We would see which category George fell into. They would not disrespect his wishes.

George wrote *Beasts of Valhalla* while listening to *The Ring* on a nonstop loop through a head phone set some thirty years earlier. I read it to him. It held it's chops, as fine writing does. George never rereads his works but I imagined him saying, "This is pretty damned good stuff!" I held his hand as I read and the sweetest, moist warm smell that was George permeated my nostrils. I couldn't get enough of that smell.

They woke him each morning to make sure he was lucid. They asked him if he knew I was there and that I was reading to him. He'd shake his head yes and then he went back into The State. This was done while I had been sent from the room. I didn't like it but I understood about agitation.

After three days it looked promising. They were going to take him off dialysis. I was on page 253 of *Beasts*. I finally went home for a good night's sleep and to play with the dogs. When I came back the next morning I learned they would not be taking him off dialysis. Additional blood test results came back. He had contracted Legionaires Disease, too. There was something else. He was depressed. The nurses said you couldn't tell, but I could. I felt it.

I called my father. "If you want to see your friend before he dies, you should come now," I told him knowing I would be pressing George's agenda within the next 24 hours.

He came over and picked up Rachael at the airport.

Leah had patients to see and I told her to finish out her week.

Judi and Dick came.

I met with the rounds doctor. He told me that *if* George came out of this state his rehabilitation and recuperation would be long and hard and that he would be transferred to a rehab center. That in itself would kill George.

"George is an enlightened man," I proudly

informed the doctor. "He is completely aware of his situation and does not want this. None of it."

The doctor acquiesced.

*

The bridal shower was to be an East Coast cosmopolitan event. Leah and several of her bridesmaids would fly into New York from Phoenix. Friends of hers from college and high school would be arriving from various areas around the country. I was especially pleased that the bridesmaids decided to have a shower in New York as there were many of my family members that would not be able to join us for the wedding in Scottsdale the following April and this way they would be able to wish her well. Most of my siblings had not even seen Rachael or Leah in many, many years.

Rachael was her maid of honor. She ran a tight ship and organization was the order of the day. She had requested that I coordinate centerpieces with her father's wife, Judy. Pleased that Judy had been included in the festivities I happily complied. The theme was a tea party. Judy had come up with a fabulous idea of using clear large glass teapots with blooming lotus flowers floating inside. This would set atop a flickering light; both of which would rest on a round, thick tatami mat. Simple and elegant, we were both satisfied. And, since I'd been on the road Judy had done the leg work, too. It had never been my nature to take a back seat on a project yet this felt pluperfect.

I arrived in town two days before the event. Having previously checked with the hotel, parked The Nest in the parking lot. She was quite the site. I then set out to find an appropriate mother of the bride outfit for the luncheon. Valerie thinks everything looks *fabulous* on me but, biting my lip I bought something I thought looked fabulous and hoped the girls wouldn't find it over the top. My dear remnant friend from downstate, Sonia, took me for a major tune up. After months on the trail I looked like a truck driver. My hair, which had gotten a bad chop somewhere outside of Anthony Chabot, had made me look like a cross between Joan of Arc and PeeWee Herman. Thank goodness it had grown in enough for 'Sonia's girl' to work her magic. I had my nails gelled, my eyebrows shaped, my lip waxed. By the time the planes landed I was good to go.

Anyone interested got massages on Friday during the day. Mimi and Paul held a beautiful welcome dinner for the out-of-towners and family members who would not be at the shower, mostly the guys and that beautiful Genevieve. They really put out the dog! I stayed in a room with Rachael and Leah Friday night at the hotel and did not ache for The Nest; it felt great to be with my girls.

Saturday morning Judy and I met up with the bridesmaids at the designated room and arranged the centerpieces. Each place setting held a contemporary small white tea cup and saucer, five tea bags, each imprinted and wrapped in ramie, a tiny silver spoon with a heart on its handle, bells and heart-shaped chocolates wrapped in small organza bags and a brightly colored imprinted napkin. There were small high gloss bags for everyone to transport their loot home in. Rachael was deliciously relaxed after having done all she could in preparation for the day. To recount the shower is to recount the tradition we all know so well. Leah showed up on cue, joyous and ebullient she took her seat on the big white wicker chair. The guests chatted, ate, played games, and then Leah opened presents; oohing and aahing appropriately, happy to be the center of attention and loving all the love she received. I made my usual quota of social faux pas which the girls tucked away in their memory banks for late night snickering and then, in the blink of an eye, it was over.

After everyone had left the bridesmaids, Rachael, and Leah ushered all of Leah's new booty to the entrance of the hotel. While this was happening I'd left to get The Nest, driving her up the palatial like circular driveway of The Crossroads and stopping in front, I opened the door of The Nest to receive the beauties and the loot. With Travis Tritt blaring *Will You Go With Me*, the girls filed in whooping and laughing; tickled pink that Leah's mom had taken to the road. We stacked up the gifts and danced in the 'living room', enjoying the high dudgeon of it all.

We all stayed in the hotel one more night. Jeff bought everybody dinner. There was late night dancing in the bar and I boogied like a maniac until the ungodly hour of 11:30, at which point I retired to our room, which by then looked like a bomb had been dropped on it – shoes clothes and girlie toiletries had been strewn all over the place. Ah, yes, a good time was had by all.

*

The nurse that had been assigned to George was not one I had met before and having to remove all of the connections between George and the equipment that had been so deliberately joined to him in order to save his life clearly went against her grain. There was a good deal of mutterings and heavy handedness during the procedure.

"This must be very difficult for you," I said,

sitting at George's side, holding his hand.

"*Very* difficult," she assured me through pursed lips.

"I need this to be as calm and loving as possible, for George's sake. Do you understand?" I barely spoke above a whisper.

"Yes," she answered humbly. She continued to work trying her best.

The doctor had told me that after George was taken off the machines he would become aware for a short period of time before the morphine took effect. During that time he would be able to hear and respond to everything around him.

Rachael, my father, Judi and Dick were at the foot of his bed.

I stood next to the side rail getting as close as I could to be sure he could see me when he woke. My legs were like rubber and I was frightened I would wet myself.

Shortly he stirred. His eyes opened, rheumy and unfocused.

"Hello, my darling," I smiled at him, my eyes filled with the same love and adoration I'd had for him since I was a child.

He gagged.

"I love you *so much*" I told him gently.

He tried to speak but the tubing that had been removed from his throat must have made it too difficult.

"I'm so proud of you, my love. You've done great."

He attempted to speak again. It was three syllables. I think he said, "I love you."

"My fine, fine man. I love you, my darling."

"We love you, George." I think that was Judi.

Other voices murmured sweetly behind us "We love you, George."

I could hear them leaving the room behind me and crying in the hall.

He tried to reach up to me and I held his other hand. "Yes, my darling. Yes. I love you so much."

"I love you." His voice was garbled and gravelly, but I could make out the words.

"I *know* you do! You're the best husband in the whole world, and I'll be loving you *always*."

"I love you," he told me again.

I continued to stoke his arm and face gently, leaning over him. "I'm so proud of you, George. My Great Love. I am so proud of you and I love you so very much."

The morphine began to take effect and he was unable to say more. He began to thrash around a bit and I was afraid he was in pain. I asked the nurse. "Is he in discomfort?"

"Maybe," she said watching his movements, "but I can't give him more morphine

without approval from the doctor."
"Then *get* it," I hissed.
I continued to stroke him and eventually sat down in a chair aside him while still holding his hand, whispering of our love and his good life. The doctor had told me that they did not expect him to live very long, maybe an hour or so, but after two hours I told Dick and Judi, Rachael and my dad to go home and I would call them. That's how George and I were, after all. We would be alone with each other to the end.
For the next eight hours George's body fought to stay alive. When his oxygen levels dropped permanently into the 50's I knew he had left, but I stayed and held him while alternately his heart and lungs failed and restarted themselves with the help of the other. Despite the fact that the sound had been turned off in the room, I could hear the monitors blaring at the nurses' station. His heart had stopped. The beeping was like that you hear standing next to a fire station, it seemed so loud to me. His lungs had stopped. Beeping burning in my ears again. I left his side for a moment to ask the nurse to turn down the sound. She looked at me sadly. There was no volume that had been turned up. It was me. It was all in my head.
I went back to the room and sat down, reminding myself that George was gone,

only his body was struggling.
It took eight hours for the battle to wage until finally the war was over.
After eight hours of struggling George ceased to exist.
I got up from his bedside and went to the nurses' station. They assured me that there was no paperwork to fill out, nothing else to be done. At 2 a.m. on November 18th I walked down the long dark corridor of ICU, stopping dead in my tracks only once contemplating racing back to his bedside and throwing myself upon him. But I knew he was gone and I commanded myself to continue down the corridor.

*

Leah had taken the week after her shower off so that we could travel together in The Nest. I couldn't have been more pleased. She had told me that she didn't want to spend most of the days on the road, so we had decided to take three or four hour drives, stop for a few days, and then continue on. The first day we would go as far as Cape May, New Jersey and spend two nights there before taking the Lewes Ferry into Delaware. We would continue down the coastline, stopping at Assateague Island to see the wild ponies. From there arrangements had been made to stay at an RV Resort (if such a term can really exist) in

Virginia Beach. A few days later I would drive Leah to the airport in Norfolk, Virginia before continuing south alone.

I had been assured when I had made reservations at various RV stops that the weather would be much milder than that of New York since we were on the coast and more southerly. The Lewes Ferry Line and The Chesapeake Bay Bridge Authorities, both, had advised me that I was approved to travel via their venues despite having 77 pounds of propane 'on board'. They just made sure I knew that the tank had to be tightly shut.

Although I still didn't seem to be able to arrange anything more than two weeks in advance for myself, I was becoming more comfortable with this mind-set and even embraced it saying, "I don't *know* what I'll want to do in two weeks. We'll see what develops." But since Leah had set aside vacation time and needed to make flight arrangements home, it was necessary to have made these plans well in advance.

And you know what they say about the best laid plans.

We arrived in Cape May just in time to greet Hurricane Ida. What a splendid conductor of a hurricane she was; orchestrating the winds and waves to her melodies of destruction. For two days Leah and I rocked back and forth in The Nest, alone in a desolate RV park; surrounded only by empty vessels abandoned for the seasons. We started a game of Gin Rummy we decided to rename Airport Rummy, meaning we would continue to play hands and carry the score for the entire week. Whoever had the highest score before we left for the airport 'won.' We also played Yahtzee, with the same idea in mind. Leah and I shared a passion for cooking. Having surpassed my talents years prior, I'd often defer to her but we both enjoyed sharing tips on making good dishes better. It was great fun planning meals and snacks together and working side by each in the tiny kitchen, glasses of wine in hand.

When The Lewes Ferry had been cancelled until further notice Leah's eyes got as big as a saucers and when they called for an evacuation of the island, I knew our plans would have to be altered. While I had great confidence in The Nest, having crossed Continental Divide in a snow storm after all, Leah was less sure. And, of course I couldn't be absolutely *certain* without doubt we would be o.k. Erring on the side of caution we felt it was time to abandon ship.

We stuffed clothes, booze and snacks into a few bags, and grabbing the Yahtzee game and a deck of cards before heading out, we hastily left The Nest in her now soggy spot. Maxine transported us to Congress Hall.

Ten minutes later we were checking in, having gone from the ridiculous to the sublime. Congress Hall was a fabulous old hotel that, due to the time of year and the stormy weather, we were fortunate enough to get a room in without having made a reservation. Boasting a spa and two restaurants it was located in the heart of the little town; surrounded by the specialty shops and quaint walkways Cape May is so well-known for. We quickly forgot about our previous life back in the humble RV park and fell right into stride with our fellow high hats. It was a deliciously decadent two days spent shopping, getting massages, dining on finely prepared meals and watching Ida rage on the beach from a safe distance - through the glorious picture window of our room.

Leah talked about her most beloved fiancé, Rory, her plans for the wedding, concerns at work and play – for my girl does work and play hard. I shared much about George and my past, telling her, as I had shared with Rachael a few months back, that in many ways her father and my divorce was more difficult even than George's death. Divorce was the death of many of the values and ideals I had held so tightly throughout most of my life, as well as the loss of our love. It had been an extremely painful and mournful time and it had involved making a choice. George's death, while not easier, was at least simpler. It was a loss of great love. There was no choice. Period.

I also shared with her that I had been extremely fortunate in my life to have had two wonderful husbands. It felt good to say that. More importantly, it felt good to *feel* that.

By the time the hurricane had subsided enough for us to leave the island we were ready to move on. The Nest, none the worse for wear, started right up and we proceeded to disembarkation at The Lewes Ferry, all atwitter at getting the front spot and a bird's eye view of The Atlantic Ocean. It was The Nest's first ferry ride and I'd say she enjoyed it grandly. We rode through the steely grey of sky and water and were deposited onto the tar-covered sands of Lewes - on time and as advertised. Unfortunately, it was still raining and miserable so we took a pass on going to Assateague Island and opted to head straight through Delaware and into Virginia in the hopes that we would be far enough south to enjoy some good weather.

The Sun Gods were not with us. Rains and

unseasonably cold weather continued until the last day of Leah's vacation. That Sunday was warm and generous. It was bright and calm. Even the RV campgrounds looked inviting. Her flight was at seven. We needed to be at the airport by six. At 12:30, all packed and prepared to leave, we loaded up Maxine and headed for the beach on the main drag of Virginia Beach, found a cozy spot for ourselves in an open sports bar on the water and watched football all afternoon. Both of us avid fans, we threw back a couple of brewskies and ordered a few snacks as we thoroughly enjoyed the game together.

Kisses and hugs later, we said our goodbyes and she left to go back home to Rory and Scottsdale.

*

I remember so clearly sitting on the bench outside St. Peter's Hospital at 2:15 a.m. on Tuesday, November 18th. I was waiting for my dad and Rachael to gather me up and bring me home. I remember staring out into the well lit parking lot, now void of visitor's cars it held only the vehicles of the hospital workers on their first shift. I remember thinking about what I should do next. Wanting to think. Wanting to plan. Using my little computer brain to problem solve so that it might occupy every corner of my

being. As always, the little bugger served me well.
It said, "We will sit *shiva.* Jewish mourning is so civilized. We'll have a few family and friends over each night for a couple of nights. Rachael will make calls and help you clean up the house and prepare some food. Send dad home. He'll come back with Ruth on Wednesday night. Call Judi in the morning and see if she will come with you to the funeral home. George will be cremated, as was his desire, and at some later date we'll spread his ashes on The Hudson. Don't forget to call Mel in case he wants to let the media know."
When Judi had come to say her goodbyes to her brother the day before I'd asked her how she wanted to mourn. Although she and Dick were active in their church – the church that their family had belonged to for over sixty years – she'd told me that she wanted to honor her brother's memory by *not* having a service for him. I reminded her that mourning was for the living and I wanted her to be comfortable in having had an opportunity to do just that; in a way that was meaningful for her. I told her that I would be there for her in whatever capacity she wanted. She had shaken her head thoughtfully and said that she thought my idea of having friends over for the next few

days sounded like something George would have loved.

For the next four days Rachael cleaned, helped me prepare, welcomed guests, spoke with those who were unattended to and slept with me on George's side of the bed. The memory of so loving an experience could not have happened without her. I placed pictures of George at various stages of his life on our oaken table. The table we had our lunch at every day; the best seat in the restaurant with only two chairs that faced our tiny corner of The Hudson. I put out a few of his books. I lit the candle inside a purple geode that my most treasured sister, Leslie, brought up for me. I put the flowers Val and Jerry sent up on the table as well. It was simple and sweet and I could have just imagined how George would compliment me on my wonderful homemaker's touch.

During the days the deer came; one wiggled his ears at me the way George used to. The turkey vultures trotted down our driveway en masse making garbling noises and arguing amongst themselves about the news. I ruefully laughed at them. At the water's edge atop the grand maple, now void of its leafy garb, a great bald eagle perched. Through the binoculars I could see him staring proudly ahead, with white wisps of hair on the nape of his neck blowing in the

winds. I thought it was George saying 'hello' to me. His presence was, indeed, absent everywhere.
Some of his classmates came by. The fellows who had extended our home stopped in. The Postmistress, Susan, and my pal from The Grand Union, Patty, offered their condolences. George's nieces, nephews, and their children were of great comfort to me those days, as were Dick and Judi. Then there was my family. My huge, loving family that, no matter how often I declined invitations to go down state and see them for various events, drove *hours* to be with me that week. The local paper wrote a fabulous piece about George, as did The Washington Post, which was then picked up by the other national papers. The web site was crazy with activity; Hunter who ran the site kept me abreast of all the many articles that were being written. I printed them all out and started a scrapbook.
I had a crystal necklace with a few of George's ashes made up for myself. I wore his favorite black ring, his high school ring and it would be many months before I was able to take his watch – the watch he had handed to me to hold for him in the emergency room that last week - off my wrist.
Leah flew in with Rory. Andrew came in,

too. We five had Thanksgiving Dinner together. And then they went home. I cried and cursed. Woe to the loving individual who tried to reach out to me; I licked my wounds and howled like a fox caught in a trap. Unable to free myself and unable to sit in the pain, I bled.

*

Leah and I'd had a great time together and I appreciated it all the more knowing that once she got married and started a family of her own this type of excursion wouldn't be in the cards for us anymore. However, I knew that new experiences would be, so I tried not to be too melancholy about her departure.

I drove from Virginia into North Carolina. My destination was Raleigh. In two days I would pick up, Syd; having reunited with her by phone after my visit with Janie and Carl she had gleefully agreed to join me. We had planned to drive through Charleston, Savannah and St. Augustine together sightseeing and touring through the south at our leisure before heading to her home in the Fort Lauderdale area of Florida. In two days. Two of the longest and hardest days I was to have on the road. It was November 18th. One year since George had died. Alone with my thoughts in a rather desolate state campground I sat, first stunned that time had gone by so quickly, then terrifically depressed. I became introspective and in looking back recalled how painstakingly slow each day had unfolded when he first died. It was the oddest sensation to have treated George's death the same way I'd treated the birth of each of my girls. When the new baby came I'd say, "She's one whole day old now... She's one week old now... She's a month old now." Each cyclical marker of time impressed the newness of the experience upon me. And so it had been with George's death; the only difference, of course, was that I had felt as if I was walking through sludge, barely able to breathe. And, now here it was one year later. Everybody says one year is a big turning point. I hoped so. My tears could still burn hot, but I had to admit they were not as hot as they had been in the beginning. I recalled how after six months I was certain that I had cried every tear I had and that surely no more could come – but they did. They just didn't come down as often. One year. What did it mean? Nothing felt different. It was still hard to move forward. Well, maybe a little bit easier. Pushing myself to put one foot in front of the other, I had been content to be diverted with people, places and things, but was that all they were, diversions? Maybe each person I'd spent time with had been healing me and I was just too close to the situation to see it. Perhaps I would look back further down the line and see it clearly. I liked to think I had offered others some goodness to enrich their lives by my presence; surely I should open my heart and accept that same gift from them. I would try to be a better receiver. And, certainly I was not as alienated from others as I'd felt when I started out in The Nest.

Then I thought about my future. Maybe in my travels I might come across a place that would speak to me as being a place of power and I could settle down. Maybe I might never find such a place and just continue to live out my remainder years on the planet 'surfing' in The Nest. Maybe I would meet someone to share my life with again. I would like that.

Despite the fact that I had cursed George so many times after he'd died for forcing me out of my comfortable life with him, my life had changed forever and now after molting and morphing a new form was beginning to emerge. I could see I had slowed down, I wasn't running so hard anymore. Also, the experience of the death of my beloved had enriched my compassion for others who had gone through the same sorrow as well as made me grateful for the preciousness and precariousness of every living creature sure to meet its end. I reminded myself that the pain of loss was commensurate with the greatness of the love. I was grateful for that. I hurt plenty, but the future would hold many choices and possibilities as long as I continued to heal myself and was open to receive them. Mostly I could feel gratitude for the opportunity to be *able* to discover what I might do for my next trick. Gently but firmly, I slipped my wedding band off the ring finger my left hand and transferred it to the pinkie finger on my right hand. It felt strange and it looked odd but it fit perfectly.

www.ingramcontent.com/pod-product-compliance
Lightning Source LLC
Chambersburg PA
CBHW030914090426
42737CB00007B/185
9781930253186